AUTHORITY IN THE CHURCH

The Place of Authority in Christ's Church

and

The Use of the Rod and Staff

A Neglected Aspect of Shepherding

Jay E. Adams

MID-AMERICA
INSTITUTE FOR NOUTHETIC STUDIES

Institute for Nouthetic Studies, a ministry of Mid-America Baptist
Theological Seminary, 2095 Appling Road, Cordova, TN 38016
mabts.edu and nouthetic.org

ISBN: 978-1-949737-80-6 (Print)
ISBN: 978-1-949737-81-3 (eBook)

Editor: Donn R. Arms

Library of Congress Cataloging-in-Publication Data
Names: Adams, Jay E., 1929 - 2020
Title: *Authority in the Church*
Jay E. Adams
Description: Cordova: Institute for Nouthetic Studies, 2025
Identifiers: ISBN 9781949737806 (paper)
Classification: LCC BV652.1.A4 | DDC 253.5

Published in the United States of America

TABLE OF CONTENTS

The Use of the Rod and the Staff

FOREWORD

Since the time of Adam, his descendants have chaffed under God's authority. It was true of Israel, God's chosen people, and it has been true of the church, God's elect. Rejection of authority invariably leads to problems and chaos. Jay Adams shows us how a Biblical understanding of authority can bring joy and peace to His people.

This book brings together two shorter books Jay Adams published shortly after he retired from pastoral ministry. In the first, *The Place of Authority in Christ's Church*, he explains what Biblical authority is and how believers are to exercise it and live under it.

In the second book, *The Use of the Rod and Staff*, he shows how God has equipped His leaders, elders and pastors, to exercise their God given authority in the church. The Biblical imagery of the Shepherd watching over and guarding his flock is instructive, and Adams encourages church leaders to both boldly and gently use the tools God has given them to lead His sheep safely to pleasant green pastures.

Donn R. Arms, editor

THE PLACE OF AUTHORITY
IN CHRIST'S CHURCH

INTRODUCTION

ONE sign of weakness in a church that otherwise might seem strong because of its numbers and wealth is the virtual absence of authority. Those in positions of authority tolerate heresy and do not confront members who live as if they were pagans; worldliness in viewpoint and methodology is the order of the day, and schism is a concept outmoded among those who view as supreme the right of the individual to defect. Yes, if you didn't know, I'm talking about today's church in America. There is something very wrong that must be addressed, dealt with, and changed, or the best of the church as we have known it for a couple of centuries past will soon disappear from the scene.

This weakness of which I speak is also clearly seen in the lack of impact that the church has upon the social, political, educational, and recreational areas of life. Millions declare their adherence to Christianity, say that they believe in the inspiration of the Bible, and hold membership in the church, but the leavening influence that they exert upon society as a whole is so minuscule that it is imperceptible. Instead, from year to year, the church becomes more and more secularized as society bears a stronger and stronger influence upon it. The church is rapidly losing its distinctiveness in a politically correct culture. Pluralism reigns. And worse still, out of ignorance, fear, and whatever other causes, the church has so adapted to this culture that even many Christian publishing houses have given way to neutral gender language, the publication of heresy such as Open Theology, and the like.

What the Reformers fought so hard to achieve, what so many of their followers gave their lives to defend, is on the verge of utter disintegration. Among so-called "evangelicals," moves are afoot to cooperate with Roman Catholics, Mormons, and others in "common causes." These risky ventures, if they go unchecked, portend serious problems for Christians in the future. Many now do not know what they ought to believe, others wonder about the validity of old distinctions, and some are toying with even greater union efforts based upon supposed secondary "agreements." Increasingly, tolerance for everything but true biblical intolerance is gaining the upper hand – even in some denominations that in the past have been known as staunchly biblical.

Why have these things happened? In the book, *The Use of the Rod and the Staff: A Neglected Aspect of Biblical Shepherding*, I show that the elders of the church have been shamefully negligent in pursuing their God-given duties, notably in protecting the flock from heretics, schismatics, and the like. This problem is not a uniquely modern phenomenon; it has persisted throughout the history of the church. In spite of explicit warnings from Paul, Peter, John, and other New Testament writers (not to mention Jesus, Who spoke of those who would come as "wolves in sheep's clothing"), elders have been delinquent in wielding the rod to drive away those who would devour the flock.

But there is a related issue that may explain in part why so many elders fail to stand between predators and their flocks: they do not recognize the authority that Jesus Christ has placed in their hands, or what is worse, they recognize it but fail to avail themselves of it. Surely any call to elders to wake up to the facts, to take up and use their weapons to ward off those who would intrude into Christ's flocks, and to assist in turning the current direction of things, must reemphasize the biblical warrant for such action. That warrant lies in the *authority* that Christ gave to His church.

Chapter 1

What's the Problem, Anyway?

Let's face it: people don't like authority. The mobs of protesters who follow the heads of countries around the world in order to "demonstrate" are, perhaps, the most visible evidence of this spirit of rebellion against authority in our day. They are composed of various groups: people who have failed to get their way by peaceful means such as legislation; people who would like to upset certain governments (or their leaders) because of their ideologies; and those who simply advocate anarchy. In addition, Libertarianism has been gaining popularity in this country, and to a slightly greater extent, there are those who would completely do away with most governmental functions. It is true that government has intruded into areas that were never intended by our founding fathers to be its venues, and has assumed an all-too-pervasive and powerful place in the life of the average citizen. This intrusive nature of government has gone a long way toward providing fuel to energize those who would like to eliminate government altogether.

But coming closer to home, even in the church, it is easy to detect the inroads of egalitarian thinking—most members speak and act as if Christ ordained no special office and granted no authority to exercise it. Even the officers themselves have so denuded their office that one would never know that Jesus expects the elders of the church to rule and teach authoritatively. Too many preachers, for instance, speak of wanting to "share" the gospel, or some other biblical truth. Share?—what a weak word! No one ever nailed anyone to the door for "sharing." Now, when one affirms, teaches, declares, proclaims, or preaches, that is a different matter. He is standing behind what he says without weakening it. But to share…? You may share an opinion, perhaps. You may offer your share of something to another, thereby indicating that you intend to offer only a part to him. But to share the gospel? Who wants only a *part* of the gospel? Preachers should present the *whole* message. Otherwise, it is no longer the gospel.

When one shares a piece of pie with someone, he doesn't give him the entire pie; only a slice. When a pastor calls on the congregation to share something with him, he thereby levels everyone to the same non-office. His message, far from being authoritative, is viewed as only a slice of the whole, which supposedly is held by the congregation. Every member's opinion carries the same weight. It places the office of teaching elder on the same plane with those who hold no office at all. In other words, any authority that the office of elder carries with it is erased by *sharing*. The office of elder has also been denuded by feminist ideology, which leads to deliberate mishandling of the Scripture, thus further weakening it. When will men begin once again to preach, herald, proclaim, and declare the Word of God authoritatively instead of sharing?

Even in so-called Bible-believing churches, few recognize that the elder has been given authority to rule and manage the church. If an elder were to confront a member about persisting in sin (as he should), even in the kindest, most helpful manner, the response is likely to be "Who is he to tell me what to do? Humph!"

The democratization of the church, which Jesus did not intend to be a democracy but a theocracy in which He is the supreme Lord and King, has been running apace. It is almost to the point where, instead of a teacher preaching the authoritative Word, the congregation thinks it has the right to determine the will of God for itself. That sad departure from biblical church government has gone so far that in many congregations any elder would hardly dare to speak of exercising authority in cases that require church discipline—if, of course, he were even to think of doing so. People bristle and become stiff-necked when they are told that they are to bear the yoke and submit to the authority of Christ.[1]

This lack of authority cries out for change. While at one time some may have misused the power Christ granted in the church, and some may have reacted against that misuse, that is no excuse for ignoring, neglect-

---

1   The persons described in the Bible as "stiff-necked" are those who, like oxen, resist being yoked to one another and to the cart. They stiffen their necks and make it difficult for the farmer to hitch them up. People who resist Christ's laws and the authority that He has given to the eldership are equally stiff-necked. They too make things difficult for the elders.

ing, or defying His authority when it is rightly exercised. Nevertheless, today it is virtually missing from the church. The pendulum has swung so far to the other side that one wonders when it will ever return.

For an elder to speak to anyone in the church in an authoritative manner is almost unheard of. Yet think—if Christ has granted authority to those who hold the office of elder, they ought to exercise that authority when necessary. They are negligent if they do not do so. And consequently, the whole church suffers.

"But," says an elder, "If I speak to anyone with authority, they will think that I am pushing myself forward. They'll assume that I think I'm a holier-than-thou. I don't even dare to preach in the second person. I have to say 'we' rather than 'you.'"

"Oh? And what will Christ think if you say 'you'? Indeed, what does He think when you know you should, but you don't?"

"Well…"

"Yes. Think about that. Doesn't God want you to speak authoritatively? 'We' preaching is almost on a level with 'sharing.' Consider this: God has granted authority to the church, but He has also granted authority to the state. You drive through a red light and are pulled over. The officer who stops you doesn't say, 'We went through a red light, so let's look at our licenses' as you both pull them out. 'We are going to pay a fine.'"

"No way!"

"Well, what does he say?"

"He says, '*You* went through a red light, let me see *your* license, and *you* are going to pay a fine.'"

"You'd better believe it! He speaks with authority. And you accept his using the second person 'you,' don't you?"

"Well, yeah. But I'm not happy about the ticket I get."

"Of course you aren't, but you don't see any self-assertion in his use of the words 'you' and 'your' *per se*, do you?"

"No, I guess not. He has the authority of the state behind him, so he can speak with authority."

"Exactly. And Paul made it clear in Romans 13 that the authority of God is backed by the state's authority (see also John 19:11). And whose authority do you have backing you?"

"The authority of God?"

"You got it right in one! Why should you be hesitant when you know that God has given you authority to exert it when necessary and proper to do so?"

"Well, nobody recognizes that authority. I guess that's why."

"And how can that sad situation be remedied? By elders copping out?"

"Well… No."

"Then one way to begin to reestablish authority in the church is to preach about it authoritatively, and to begin to use it in the exercise of church discipline."

The truth of the matter is that many elders are simply "chicken"; they are afraid to assert the authority that Christ has given to them. They ought either to begin to do so or to resign from their office. Christ's church needs more courageous elders; there are too many wimps! Seminaries ought to teach about the authority of the eldership, and presbyteries and other ecclesiastical bodies ought to back those who practice it. It is time for the church to awaken to its responsibilities.

CHAPTER 2
WHAT IS "AUTHORITY"?

IT is probably necessary to say just a bit about what the word "authority" means in the context in which we are using it in this book. Most people have some notion about the meaning and use of the term, but if they were called upon to define it, they would be hard-pressed. We shall begin by taking a look at two Greek words that will help us understand what is meant. The first of these is *dunamis*. This word, from which the English word "dynamite" was derived, carries the idea of power that enables one to accomplish something. There is a child's joke that goes like this: "What do you feed a 500-pound gorilla?" Answer: "Anything he wants!" That's *dunamis*! It is the power that one has, by reason of importance or might, to influence others in order to obtain what he wishes. In that sense, "authority" comes from the ethos that one's physical (or other sorts of) personal power provides. In the case of Jesus Christ, it may refer to one's personal, moral weight. It may be an authority that is valid or invalid before God. But it is, nevertheless, authority at its rawest level.

Another Greek word that is important to our discussion is *exousia*. This second term refers to one's right to do something: a right that others have conferred upon him. It is the kind of authority that the policeman in the previous chapter exerts when he stops a motorist to present him with a speeding ticket. He wears a uniform, which symbolizes the power and force of the entire state that backs him up in what he is doing. The state that issued him his trooper's uniform, badge, and gun did so in order to confer upon him the right to act on its behalf within the limits of his office.

When a man is elected to be an elder and hands are laid upon him, by this act, the church confers the office upon him with all its responsibilities and rights. From that time forward, he has been commissioned by God through His church to carry out the tasks the Bible has assigned. Heaven backs him up as he faithfully discharges those duties (Acts 18:18-20).

The individual who wears the trooper's uniform may not be the kind of person who has much personal *dunamis*. That is to say, he may not exemplify what the office stands for in his own person. He may cheat on his wife, be a very poor father, have an ungovernable temper, and the like. But unless he is found guilty of behavior unbecoming an officer of the law, he retains his conferred authority (*exousia*) and may exercise it when dealing with the public. And the public must recognize and respect his authority and obey him.

Preachers and other elders may not fit their uniform snugly either. They may fail to work diligently in the preparation of sermons, they may neglect their parishioners, and so on. But until removed from office for cause, they still retain their *exousia*. Since all are imperfect sinners, the task of the elder is to grow more and more in terms of his personal *dunamis* so that he fills out the uniform that God issued to him. In the Lord Jesus Christ we see the two in perfect correspondence with one another. In Him alone can we see what it means for *exousia* and *dunamis* to meet, each in its fullest.

As they say in the army, "Salute the uniform, not the man." This should be less true of the elder than of a soldier since God has set forth a higher standard of qualifications for the elder (see Titus 1; 1 Timothy 3). The goal for all elders is to become, in their personal lives, people whose internal *dunamis* measures up to the external *exousia* conferred upon them.

There was an authority that Jesus had with others by virtue of His presence among them. They recognized that there was something about what He did and the way in which He spoke that exhibited an *exousia* that grew out of His *dunamis*. Here is what we read:

> *Now the result was that when Jesus finished these sayings, the crowds were astonished at His teaching since He taught them as an authority and not as their scribes* (Matthew 7:28, 29).

The word "authority" in verse 29 is *exousia*. Literally, the phrase in the original reads, "as one having *exousia*." From His personal *dunamis*, people concluded that He was like a person upon whom authority to teach had been conferred.[1] The assessment of Christ here is extraordinary. By the very words that He spoke (content) and the way in which he spoke them (manner), people concluded that Jesus had the right[2] to teach as He did. While He had never had men confer authority upon Him, as the scribes had, nevertheless, His *dunamis*, or internal authority, was all the authority those who listened to Him needed. That *dunamis* came across to them as *exousia*. Indeed, it seems that because they so perfectly correspond to one another, His listeners could not distinguish the two kinds of authority.

So, as we have been looking at these two words, we have been coming to the conclusion that "authority" is the right (*exousia*) conferred upon someone to act in some specific way or ways. We have further concluded that this person's *dunamis* ought more and more to correspond to the *exousia* by which he acts. He should wear the uniform well, filling it out in all respects. In this book, while we shall emphasize *exousia*, we shall also have occasion from time to time to speak of the need for *dunamis* among officers of the church, who represent the heavenly government. It is good to fix the import of each word in your mind before turning to the next chapter.

---

1   Of course, this was true. At His baptism Jesus received authority from God for His work.
2   *Exousia* is frequently translated "right," referring to the authority that has been conferred upon someone to do something (see also the use of *exousia* in 1 Corinthians 9:4-12)..

CHAPTER 3

LOOKING AT JESUS' *EXOUSIA*

WE saw how the crowds who heard Jesus speak responded. They attributed *exousia* (conferred authority) to Him[1] , although He refused to accept the title of Rabbi, which would have meant that he had received such authority from the Sanhedrin. Yet Jesus did have authority—*divinely conferred* authority. It is that power that we will explore in this chapter.

In Luke 5, verses 17 through 26, we have the account of Jesus' healing of the paralytic. When He said to the man, "Your sins are forgiven you" (v. 20), the Pharisees objected saying, "Who is this person who speaks blasphemies? Who, but God alone, can forgive sins?" (v. 21) To which objection Jesus responded as follows:

> *"Why are you thinking this way in your hearts? Which is easier—to say 'Your sins are forgiven,' or to say, 'Rise and walk?' Now so that you will know that the Son of Man has authority* [exousia] *on earth to forgive sins,"* He said to the paralytic, *"Get up and pick up your stretcher and go home." Immediately, he got up before them, picked up his stretcher, and went home, praising God* (Luke 5:22-24).

Plainly, Jesus declared that He possessed authority to say and do what He did. Since that authority did not issue from men, it must have come directly from God. In the discussion between Jesus and the Jews found in John 5, He declared:

> *Let me assure you that the hour is coming, and now is, when the dead will hear the voice of God's Son, and those who hear will live.[2] Just as*

---

1   See also Mark 1:22, 27; Luke 4:32.
2   The "dead" here are those who are dead spiritually whom Jesus granted spiritual life.

the Father has life in Himself, so too He has granted the Son to have life in Himself. He granted Him authority [exousia] *to pass judgment, because he is the Son of Man* (John 5:25-27).

Once again, we see how Jesus asserts that He has been "granted" the right to give life to others because the Father conferred upon Him (as man) the "authority" to do so. And in His great intercessory prayer, He reiterates the fact:

Father, the hour has come; glorify Your Son that Your Son may glorify You, since You gave Him authority [exousia] *over all flesh so that He may give eternal life to all that You gave Him* (John 17:1, 2).

There can be no doubt, then, that Jesus acted under authority duly granted to Him by the Father. That He did not act authoritatively *before* His baptism, but began to do so immediately thereafter, makes it clear that it was at that event that such authority was given to Him. The Father declared on that occasion that Jesus was His beloved Son and poured out the Spirit upon Him without measure. This event was, in effect, Jesus' installation into His mediatorial office as the Son of Man. It was the occasion on which the Father conferred upon Him all the authority of His office, only after which He went forth carrying out His mission of salvation.[3]

Finally, having carried out all that He was commissioned to do on earth, and having risen from the dead, before ascending to the mediatorial throne, Jesus said, "All authority in heaven and on earth has been given to Me" (Matthew 28:18). As the God-man, He was now about to rule over all things for the sake of His church. Paul wrote of the Father's

mighty strength that He exerted for Christ when He raised Him from the dead, and seated Him in the heavenly places at His right hand, far

---

3   This is one reason why we can know that those spurious documents that give accounts of Jesus doing miracles as a child are entirely inconsistent with the true New Testament books.

above all rule and authority and power and lordship, and every name
that is named not only in this age, but also in the coming one. He
has subjected everything under His feet and made Him Head over all
things for the sake of the church (Ephesians 1:19-22).

Here, unmistakably, Jesus is said to rule over all other powers and
authorities for the benefit of His church. His authority is preeminent.

It is worth noting that in this life and in that which follows, Jesus'
ministry is *authorized* by the Father. Until the time when that authority
was granted and conferred upon Him, He engaged in no official ministry.
After conferral, however, all that He did, He did under authority. And
even now, as the God-man, He is ruling and reigning supremely by the
special authorization of the Father Who granted Him the right to do so.

If Jesus, as the God-man, could not minister except under a grant of
authority, it is important to stress that those who minister today must
likewise be authorized to minister. There are too many who have taken
it upon themselves to minister without any authority. Speaking of the
then-unthinkable act of one taking upon himself the authority to minister in God's Name, the writer to the Hebrews pointed out that:

A person doesn't take this honor upon himself, but, on the contrary, he is
called by God just as Aaron was. So too, Christ didn't exalt Himself to
become a High Priest, but, rather, He was appointed by the One Who
said to Him, "You are My Son; I have begotten You today (Hebrews
5:4, 5).

Throughout both Testaments, we see that those ministering for God
must have been duly called and authorized. Even Jesus was subject to this
rule, as the writer observed. How, then, do some simply set themselves
up as ministers of the church of Jesus Christ without any authorization?[4]
The idea, as Hebrews 4 says, was unthinkable. Yet in our day, when there
is so little respect for authority, no such attitude prevails. People do as

---

4   And, in some cases, even in spite of the church's refusal to ordain or otherwise authorize them as ministers of the new covenant.

they please and expect that God will be pleased as well. If I have read the Scriptures rightly, He must be greatly displeased by such willful, arrogant, anarchistic action taken in His Name.

CHAPTER 4

TRANSFER OF AUTHORITY

J ESUS was given *exousia* by His Father which, as we have seen, He exercised from His baptism onwards, and which He is still exercising as the God-man on the throne of heaven today. But before He ascended, He gave some of that authority to His followers—especially to the disciples who would become apostles. At first, it seems that He granted authority to them for their early mission:

> *He appointed[1] twelve that they might be with Him and that He might send them out to preach and to exercise authority to cast out demons (Mark 3:14, 15).*

But later, when He officially organized His church, it was with a grand, authoritative act that He conferred authority to forgive sins (the same authority that we saw in the previous chapter). Jesus said:

> *Peace to you. As the Father sent Me, so also do I send you." When He had said this, He breathed on them and said to them, "Receive the Holy Spirit. If you forgive anybody's sins, they are forgiven; if you retain them, they are retained* (John 20:21-23).

The missionary work that Jesus had come to do was now transferred to His apostles, whom He sent in like manner as He had been sent by the Father. He commissioned them to do this work by breathing on them as a symbol that they were receiving the Holy Spirit as He had at His baptism. They were to proclaim the gospel, by which people's sins would be forgiven or retained according to whether or not they believed. This act, by which Jesus constituted His church, involved a transfer of authority. The apostles

---

1 Notice the authoritative language: "He appointed."

would be "sent" (as He had been) on their mission. That is, they would not speak in their own name, but would preach in the Name of the One Who sent them. It was, then, in Christ's own authority that they ministered.

In addition, Jesus gave the great commission under His universal authority (Matthew 28:20) and instituted the authoritative process of Church discipline (Matthew 18:15 and following). This process involved "binding" and "loosing," which were authoritative acts of admitting persons into and dismissing persons from membership in His church. Unless one has been officially called as an elder and set apart for that work today, he has no right to engage in this process. But where this process does not exist, it is questionable whether we can determine that a church exists. That is true because it is church discipline that draws the line between the church and the world.

Beyond any doubt, the apostles assumed the authority that Jesus had given them. In 1 Timothy 6, verses 13 and 17, for instance, Paul encouraged Timothy (an elder of the church) to "instruct with authority" and "Authoritatively instruct." The word that I have translated "authoritatively instruct" (and "instruct with authority") is *paraggello*. This word was used in the papyri to describe the "official summons before a court."[2] It carried the authoritative air of an official notice or order. Paul too writes with authority to summon Timothy to keep Christ's "commandment unspotted and free from suspicion" (1 Timothy 6:14). And then he urges Timothy, as one who had been officially ordained by the presbytery,[3] to "authoritatively instruct the rich" (v. 17). We can see from this passage that not only did the apostles receive authority for their work, but preaching elders in the church had received authority to pursue theirs as well. The New Testament ministers of the Word carried on their tasks under authority and with authority. There can be no question about that fact.

It is certain that the apostles passed down the authority to minister in Christ's Name to men who were appointed to serve as elders in

---

2   Moulton and Milligan, The Vocabulary of the Greek New Testament, p. 481.
3   1 Timothy 4:14. In 1 Thessalonians 2:4–7, Paul asserts his apostolic prerogatives even when restraining from their use.

the church. At the Jerusalem conference (Acts 15), apostles and elders from the churches gathered to determine how to handle the Judaizing tendencies that had troubled the church. After they reached a solution, we read that "As they traveled through these cities, they delivered [to the churches] the decisions reached by the apostles and the elders at Jerusalem, and told them to *obey* them" (Acts 16:4, emphasis mine). The decisions were "reached by the apostles and the elders" jointly. They had equal authority to decide upon the matters before them. Moreover, others in the churches were to "obey" these decisions because they carried the authority to require Christians to obey.

Thus, "submission" was to be given to those who served with Paul in the work of the ministry (2 Corinthians 16:15, 16). And Titus was ordered by the apostle to "speak these things; urge and convict, with recognition that you have full authority to give orders. Let nobody disregard you." The Greek New Testament term translated "full authority to give orders" is *epitage*.[4] This word was used of a commander giving orders to his soldiers. Stronger still, in this very letter, the word is used of God's "order" to Paul (Titus 1:3). Moreover, Titus is instructed not to allow anyone to "disregard" the authoritative orders that he issues. The word "disregard" is a vivid one meaning, literally, "to think around." That is to say, no one was to be allowed to avoid the orders he was giving.

Similarly, the writer of Hebrews commands:

> Obey your leaders and submit to them. They are keeping watch over your lives as men who will have to give an account. Obey so that they may do this with joy and not as a burden, since that wouldn't be to your advantage (Hebrews 13:17).

There is no doubt that these elders are under authority themselves, as well as exercising authority in the church. They will have to *give an account* of their ministry among the members of the flock. That means that they are ministering in Christ's Name (not their own) and are answerable to Him.

---

4 The Greek reads "with all authority." That is, with complete or full authority.

The authority that the apostles and the elders had was, therefore, not absolute. It was subject to the review of the Lord, Whose authority it ultimately was. Because of this, it is possible to question the authority that an elder has[5] by appealing to the written authority of the Scriptures. Elders may go wrong—and, of course, have often done so—and must be called to submit to the greater authority under which they operate.

The basic considerations that we have explored in this chapter underlie all else that I shall have to say about biblical authority, and should be kept in mind as we continue.

---

5   But not that of an inspired apostle when speaking or writing under inspiration.

CHAPTER 5

WHAT DOES AUTHORITY DO?

So far we have seen that all true authority is from God (cf. John 19:11). We have noted that Jesus has supreme authority in heaven and on earth as the God-man Who is seated at the right hand of God. We have further observed that He delegated part of His authority to the apostles who, in turn, granted a part of their authority to elders. So plenty of authority has been granted to the church; quite enough to bring about and keep good order. But is that the only purpose of this authority—to avoid chaos and anarchy?

In addition to an authoritative Book upon which to base one's thinking and action, there must be persons whose task is to authoritatively speak and counsel from it. These same persons should see to it that all things are done in accordance with that authoritative book. That certainly is one major reason for the exercise of true authority: so that all things may be done decently and in order (1 Corinthians 14:40).

But again, let us ask, are there other reasons for giving authority to the eldership? Very definitely, yes. In 2 Corinthians 10:8 and 13:10, Paul tells us:

> *Even if I should boast too much about the authority that the Lord gave us for building you up and not for tearing you down, I am not going to be ashamed of it... It is for this reason that I am writing these things while I'm absent, so that when I'm present I won't have to cut off any of you by the authority that the Lord gave me for building up and not for tearing down.*

Clearly, Paul understood that Jesus granted him authority in order to build up the saints in their most holy faith, and to build these bodies into strong congregations that would be able to withstand all that the world would throw at them. The second reason, then, is edification (or building up). Now, because he knew that in the Corinthian church there were problems standing in the way of edification, he said that he wanted to use his authority for the positive purpose of assisting them in their growth. He did not want to have to use that authority to "cut off" anyone from the congregation who might not give heed to these positive, edifying efforts. He wanted all to recognize and submit to the authority of Christ, in Whose Name he was writing. Yet the very mention of "cutting people off" from membership in the church clearly indicates that, if and when necessary, Paul would use his apostolic authority to do so.

How does authority build up Christians in their faith? If there were no authoritative writings such as those penned by the apostle, Christians would not be sure whether they ought to believe and do what the apostles or others tell them. But as it is, not only were the apostles and prophets able to write authoritatively because the Holy Spirit spoke inerrantly through them and through their writings. In doing so, they were able to reveal the deposit of the faith once-for-all delivered to the saints, and by that authority they were also able to defend it from all errors. This was done in such a manner that those who trust in Christ might have certainty about His preceptive will. Since growth and edification are a matter of knowledge of the truth translated into life, there had to be an authoritative Source of truth. According to John 17:17, sanctification (growing more like Christ) takes place through the appropriation of God's truth. In that verse, Jesus said that God's Word is "truth."

So authority helps reduce confusion and works toward order. God is a God of order Who will have all things done decently and in order. The second purpose of authority is to ensure that orderly conditions prevail so as to accomplish edification. The two purposes complement one another.

There can be little or no growth under conditions of disorder. But there is a third reason that Jesus granted authority to the apostles and the elders of His church. There was more than a hint about that third purpose in the quotation from 2 Corinthians 13:10 when Paul spoke of not wanting to find it necessary to use his authority to "cut off" members from the church. Plainly, he knew that he had the authority to do just that. The third reason, then, is, when all persuasion fails, to eliminate anyone who would create confusion, disorder, or introduce false teachings into the body.[1] Churches, and the individuals in them, cannot be built up when there are those in them whose sole efforts are exerted to tear them down!

Paul called this third use of authority "punishment," as, indeed, it was. He wrote:

> *The punishment that the majority inflicted upon this person is sufficient; so, instead of going on with that, you should rather forgive and help him, so that he won't be overwhelmed by too much pain. Therefore, I urge you to officially reaffirm your love to him* (2 Corinthians 2:6-8).

Paul was writing about the repentant man whom he had previously encouraged the church to put out of their midst. Here's what he had written about this person in 1 Corinthians:

> *Even though I am absent in body, I am present in the spirit and, as if I were present, have already made a judgment about the one who has been doing this thing. When you are assembled, and my spirit and the power of the Lord Jesus are with you, in the Name of the Lord Jesus deliver this person to Satan for the destruction of the flesh so that his spirit may be saved on the Lord's Day* (1 Corinthians 5:3-5).

This authoritative declaration indicates that Paul expected the church to punish this then-unrepentant member by cutting him off. His words are: "Clean out the old leaven" (v. 7). Plainly, then, the third purpose of authority was, as Jesus put it, to bind and loose. So edification is the fundamental positive end in view, but when disorder occurs as the result of heresy, schism, or an unrepentant lifestyle that cannot be countenanced, a negative use of authority may be needed to reestablish conditions that are conducive to edification. Actually, this sort of negative action, when properly carried out, has nothing but positive effects.

---

1   For information about protecting the flock from falsehood, see the second part of this book, *Using the Rod and the Staff: A Neglected Aspect of Biblical Shepherding*.

It is important that those who possess authority in the church strive, as Paul did, to use that authority for purposes of edification whenever possible. There are some who like to emphasize the punishing aspects of authority; Paul sought in every way to avoid that. But he did not hesitate to resort to punishment when all else failed.[2] Does your congregation practice church discipline? Or, like the Corinthian church, does it "arrogantly" (1 Corinthians 5:1-7) believe that it may deal with the problem in its own way?

---

2   There are those who think that the elder's authority is only ministerial and declarative. They do not believe that he has been granted power to legislate or to punish. Clearly, Paul thought that punishment by cutting off was a function of the eldership. And, while elders may make no laws, they have the right and obligation to legislate practical matters of good order such as when and where the congregation will meet for services.

CHAPTER 6

PROBLEMS WITH AUTHORITY

EVER since Adam fell, people have had problems with authority. There seems to be a fundamental bias against authority that manifests itself in the heart of every sinner. This bias, to put it simply, is a bias toward rebellion against God's legitimate authority. It is important to study this bias toward rebellion to see what may be done about it. There is nothing that destroys lives and congregations more than allowing this attitude to spread throughout the body. No wonder Paul referred to it as "leaven" that needed to be "cleaned out"!

Adam and Eve were the first to have a problem with authority. Since they were created good, yet capable of sinning or obeying, we do not know what it was within them that led to rebellion. The question remains, "How could a perfectly good man sin?" That is one of the few biblical questions to which Christians have no satisfactory answer. But we do know that Adam rebelled against the Word of the Lord, Who told him not to eat of the tree of the knowledge of good and evil. He pitted a usurper's *assumed* "authority" against the *true* authority of his Creator! And ever since, men have been born with a nature that is biased against rightful authority.

God's command in Genesis 2:16, 17 made the choice an issue of authority. Who was the true authority? Was it God or was it Satan? Whose word was to be trusted? Whose word was authoritative? To turn from God's word to Satan's word about the tree and its effects that it would have upon Adam, meant that he accepted the latter's word as authoritative. This act of rebellion was an act in which God was rejected as man's rightful Authority. Rejection of lawful authority and acceptance of unlawful authority is the very essence of rebellion.

Not only was there a rejection of God and an acceptance of the evil one, but Adam's action was also a bid for autonomy. *He*, rather than God, would become the final arbiter of whose word was authoritative and whose was not. *He* would be "the master of his own fate." The notion of rebellious autonomy is what has persisted in the human race, alienating man from God.

This bias for rebellion rather than for obedience seems to be so deeply embedded within the heart of man ever since Adam that it may be considered the very core sin from which all other sin flows. It is something that even believers, who have accepted God's Word about the Savior as true, still struggle with in a multitude of ways. Even after regeneration, they have difficulty accepting and following the commands of God—even though (theoretically) they know that His way is best. Sinful patterns that run deep are hard to throw off. It is not easy even for the regenerate to overcome the autonomist tendencies of the past.

This bias frequently cropped up throughout the history of Israel. Again and again we encounter a pattern of rebellion. This pattern has its most vivid expression in the stories of the golden calf and of Korah's rebellion. In these two incidents, it is interesting to examine what those in a place of authority did in dealing with the rebellion of the people. The contrast between the two occasions should be instructive to those in places of authority in Christ's church today.

When Moses went up into the mountain to receive the law, he left Aaron in charge. Because Moses did not immediately reappear, the people became impatient and determined to set up a golden calf as the god whom they would serve. This act of sheer rebellion stands as the prototype for all future rebellion against God following Adam's sin. It demonstrates that when a sinner is allowed to think that he is autonomous and fully in charge of his own life, he will set up another god in place of the true One.

The exchanges between Moses and God, and then Moses and Aaron after Moses returned, are most instructive. God described the people as "stiff-necked" (Exodus 32:9). Moses asked Aaron, "What did this people do to you that you have brought this great sin upon them?" (v. 21). Aaron's answer is pitiful: he says, "You know the people yourself, that they are prone to evil" (v. 22). He then goes on to make the miserable excuse that he threw the gold into the fire and "out came this calf" (v. 24). Rebellion leads one to offer the most ridiculous reasons to justify it.

Talk to elders in churches today who refuse to discipline members who clearly deserve it, and they too will offer lame excuses!

Moses saw that "the people were *let loose*" (a literal but quite expressive translation of verse 25, italics mine) because Aaron had not exerted his authority. Rather than stop them, Aaron had gone along with their rebellious request and "let them loose" (v. 25). The literal Hebrew expression "let them loose," says it all. Aaron allowed the people to have their own way, to act *autonomously*—*w*hich was to assert their own authority as final and, thereby, to rebel against the God of heaven. Because Aaron failed to exert his authority, about three thousand men were slain in one day (v. 28).

Here is a clear case of the dire consequences of the failure of a leader to use his God-given authority. Instead, he gave in to the people who, having been allowed to do as they pleased, immediately rebelled. Until elders recognize that this rebellious tendency to assert autonomy *will* manifest itself, and that if they allow people to be "let loose," the church will continue to suffer. It is their obligation, rather, to assert their authority to forestall such rebellion.

In the case of Korah's rebellion, once again we see the evil, rebellious heart of man manifesting itself. The difference was that Moses stood up against the rebellion, asserting his authority. The entire issue that arose had to do with authority. Korah charged Moses with going too far (Numbers 16:3). It was his contention that "all the people are holy," by which he meant equally capable of leading, and he leveled this further charge that Moses and Aaron had exalted themselves "above the assembly of the Lord" (v. 3). Dathan and Abiram also refused to heed Moses' authoritative summons. They too manifested the spirit of rebellion by their words:

> We will not come up. Is it not enough that you have brought us up out
> of a land flowing with milk and honey to have us die in the wilderness,
> but would you also lord it over us? (v. 12, 13)

This time, however, Moses did not allow the people to get out of hand. Rather, he asserted his divinely given authority and took up the challenge. In response, God demonstrated that Moses had been rightly acting in His Name by opening the ground and swallowing up Korah and his entire crowd (v. 31-33). Though He will not open the ground for you to swallow up trouble-makers, elder, you can be sure that He will acknowledge your faithful use of rightly conferred authority and bless you and your church as a result.

You would think that such a denouement to Korah's rebellion would have caused the people to fear and respect the authority of Moses. But it did not. The spirit of rebellion ran so deep that "on the next day all the congregation of the sons of Israel grumbled against Moses and Aaron" (v. 41), blaming them for the deaths of those who died when the earth opened up and swallowed them. As a result, God sent a plague among the people and nearly fifteen thousand more perished (v. 46-50). It seems that people never learn! Rebellion is firmly fixed in the heart of sinful man!

In the first of these two instances, there was a failure of authority; it was an authority crisis that allowed the people to rebel. They were "let loose" so as to do what their sinful hearts dictated. This story shows clearly the importance of authority on the part of leadership among God's people. Failure to assert authority leads to rebellion which, in turn, leads to destruction. In the other instance, rebellion was checked by the assertion of rightful authority. While it did not forestall some, the rebellion of the congregation as a whole was quelled. Yet, even then, rebellion boiled over in the hearts and words of those who had just seen the hand of God at work. As a result, God purified the people by cutting off many of those who had been rejecting His authority. From these two incidents, it is possible for elders to learn the utter importance of authority rightly exercised—if only they will!

CHAPTER 7

AN AUTHORITATIVE MESSAGE

C ERTAINLY, the messenger was authorized by the Lord to carry His message. In the first place, as we have seen, Jesus called His apostles the "sent off ones" (that is the meaning of the word "apostle"). An apostle is someone who has been sent off by another to do his bidding. Like an ambassador, he speaks, not for himself, but for the one who sent him. He is an *official, authoritative* representative of that person. This connection is so close that how people receive the messenger is considered equivalent to how they receive the sender. Jesus declared, "Whoever receives you receives Me, and whoever receives Me receives the One Who sent Me" (Matthew 10:40), thereby indicating that He too was an Apostle (sent off One) of the Father. It is clear, as we saw, that Jesus was the authorized Representative of the Father and that He, in turn, authorized His disciples to represent Him. Then, as He had done, they authorized the elders in the churches they planted to speak and act authoritatively in the Name of the Father, the Son, and the Holy Spirit.

In order to make sure that what the elders of the various churches taught remained true (since they were not inspired men as Jesus and the apostles[1] were), the apostles gave the church a "deposit" of truth that they expected the church to "guard" so as to be able to pass it down to succeeding generations. Qualified men were to be chosen for this function so that there would be no deviation from the apostolic message. Paul wrote to Timothy,

> *And the things that you heard from me before many witnesses, pass along to trustworthy persons who will be able to teach others also (2 Timothy 2:2).*

---

1   For details on the inspired preaching of the apostles, see Preaching According to the Holy Spirit. The New Testament clearly teaches that the apostles' preaching, as well as their writing, was inerrant.

It was not enough to have authorized messengers; the message itself had to be authentic. If there was a message given in a form in which it could be retained and examined, then what preaching elders proclaimed in generations to come could be compared to the deposited message to be sure that they were preaching the truth.

That is the only way in which there could have been a Reformation. The reformers questioned the authority of the clergy of their day on the basis that neither their actions nor their message squared with the "good deposit" which the apostles bequeathed to the church. The apostles left behind that "deposit," which was the authorized apostolic message, in the form of twenty-seven inspired letters and books that we call The New Testament. This valuable deposit has been taken for granted all too often in our day. Many prefer fluffy stories to the Word of God. Today, experience reigns rather than the authorized truth of a written revelation from God. And what is it that we do when we prefer someone's experience over God's Word? We set up that autonomous experience as our standard of faith and practice. It is a matter of choosing the creature over the Creator.

Giving us this deposit of His authorized truth through the inspiration of the Holy Spirit, of course, was the Lord's doing. It was not enough to ordain and authorize apostles to deposit the truth with the church. They might get it wrong. What they said and wrote had to be and remain the inspired, authentic message that they were given by God. It must not be adulterated. That is why, as Jude put it, the message was clearly known and shaped so that it could be called "the faith that was delivered to the saints in a full and final way" (Jude 3). It was in such form that it could be "delivered" to the church in one piece or package.

Paul likewise ordered Timothy to "guard that which was entrusted" to him (1 Timothy 6:20). The words "that which was entrusted" are a translation of but one term in the original Greek, *paratheke*, which means "the deposit." Souter says that the word was used for "the deposit (properly of money or valuables deposited with a friend for safe-keeping, while the owner is abroad)."[2] What an appropriate term!

---

2   Alexander Souter, A Pocket Lexicon to the Greek New Testament.

In 2 Timothy, Paul works out this figure of speech in some detail as he applies it to the depositing of the apostolic message. Here is what he had to say:

> Have [or hold to] the pattern of healthy words that you heard from me in the faith and love that are in Christ Jesus; guard the good deposit [paratheke] entrusted to you through the Holy Spirit Who dwells within us (2 Timothy 1:13, 14).

Note that Paul speaks of a "pattern of healthy words" and of "the good deposit entrusted to you." Let us examine those two ideas. First, there was a deposit that was eminently "valuable," more valuable than money or jewels. It was God's truth which He graciously gave to His church through authorized messengers. This truth consisted of the gospel message and all that flowed from it. Literally, the phrase "the good deposit entrusted to you" in the Greek is but two words: "my deposit." What does that mean?

Think of someone depositing money at the window of a bank. He could speak of that which he is depositing as "my deposit." That is the idea conveyed by the King James Version of verse 12 and the hymn based upon it: "that which I have entrusted unto Him against that day." But the words "my deposit," used in these verses, could be taken another way. The teller who receives the money that is deposited may also speak of that money as "my deposit." It is now *entrusted* into his hands to *guard* on behalf of the one who deposited it. And, from the context, one can readily see that it is that second thought which the apostle Paul had in mind.

When he spoke of His deposit, Paul thought of the deposit which God had given to him (v. 12) that must be "guarded" all the way up "until" the last day. And when he spoke of passing that deposit on to Timothy, he referred to that "deposit" of truth in terms of a "pattern of healthy [sound] words" that he entrusted to him (v. 14). Because it was an exceedingly valuable deposit that he was leaving with him, he urged Timothy to "guard" it.

So it was important for the apostle to leave a "deposit" in a form (pattern) that was easily retained and passed on to "trustworthy persons" who would be "competent to teach others also." This was the method by which the authorized message was to be preserved throughout the centuries until the last day. Paul deposited the message with Timothy (as did the other apostles chosen to write inspired material) in the form of a pattern of healthy words that he handed over to him in written form. Thus, the "good deposit" has been preserved for us in the writings of the New Testament.

All of these precautions to preserve a "deposit" and to pass on "a pattern of healthy words" indicate that the message was understood to be in a form that was depositable. It was to be preserved intact in that form. Clearly, that was what Paul had in mind when he urged Timothy to *guard* the message as something valuable. He wanted him to pass on the "authoritative" message without alteration.

If there had not been a message that was in a written form which it was possible to maintain, then it would be subject to much change through the years. And we see that when people or churches departed from the authorized form of the message as it was given in the New Testament, that is exactly what happened. As Rome departed from a scriptural base, over the years she turned more and more to extraneous accretions. This continued until, in time, it was impossible to discern the "good deposit." Untrustworthy men over the years had received the good deposit, left the original pattern in which it was found in the Bible, and distorted it beyond recognition. At the time of the Reformation, the gospel and other teachings of the apostles could not be found in the official doctrines of the Roman church. Instead, the church trusted in extraneous ideas that came from various other sources, most of which were pagan.

But because there was a written form in which the "deposit" had been preserved, the reformers were able to scrape off the many accretions and return to the simple, saving truths that are so clearly taught in the Bible. We may thank God that "through the Holy Spirit Who dwells within us," the authorized message is still available to us today. And elders and the members of the church should not only guard that written deposit of truth, but cherish it.

So authority extends not only to the messengers who were chosen to proclaim the gospel, but also to the message which Paul was so earnestly concerned to preserve in its authoritative form. Respect for the Bible, then, ought to be uppermost in the hearts of all of God's people.

CHAPTER 8
THE SCRIPTURES AS AN AUTHORITY

THERE are those who debate the idea that the Scriptures are authoritative. As a cover for their unbelief, they piously claim that one can attribute authority to God alone. They call those who say that God exercises His authority over His church through authorized persons, who are committed to understanding and following the Bible, adherents to a "paper Pope." Does the Bible represent itself as the Source of authority for the life of the church in general and for the Christian's life in particular? In other words, is the Bible *the* authoritative Word from God, and if so, how does it function in such a capacity?

In addition to the concept of an authoritative, divinely-deposited Message, which we explored in part in the previous chapter, what does the Bible have to say about itself? Let's begin with the gospel—the fundamental message, which, by believing, justifies a sinner before God. In 1 Corinthians 15:1-4, Paul set forth the two points of the good news this way:

> *Now I want to remind you, brothers, of the good news that I announced to you … through which also you are saved … I delivered to you as of the greatest importance what I also received, that Christ died for our sins, in agreement with the Scriptures, and that He was buried, and that He was raised on the third day in agreement with the Scriptures.*

Notice two facts. First, Paul "received" the good news from God. It was not something that he heard from men (cf. Galatians 1:1). One might say, in the words of the last chapter, that the gospel message was "deposited" with him. It was "revealed." Secondly, Paul confirmed this gospel message as being from God by comparing it with the Old Testament Scriptures. As he put it, it was "in agreement with the Scriptures."[1] The Scriptures, he implied by saying so, were the authority by which one could determine whether or not a message was true. Clearly, Paul's double mention of scriptural agreement indicates that he was appealing to them as the final authority. If something was in agreement with the Scriptures, it was from God; it was true. This appeal to the authority of the Bible was typical of all of the Old Testament quotations found in the New Testament which were used to support what one wrote.

For instance, on one occasion, Jesus cited a biblical reference as the authority for what He was teaching and then added, "the Scripture cannot be broken"[2] (John 10:34, 35). By that short, but pregnant, comment, He pointed out that the Bible is inerrant – the final authority on all issues. As the Bible was the authority for Paul, it was also for Jesus. On another occasion, He declared that those people who opposed His message were "mistaken" because they didn't know the Scriptures (Matthew 22:29).

In Luke 16:19—31, we read the account of the rich man and Lazarus. At the conclusion of the story, here is the significant observation that Abraham made:

> But Abraham said, "They have Moses and the Prophets;[3] let them hear them." But he [the rich men] said, "No, father Abraham. But if somebody from the dead goes to them, they will repent." Then he [Abraham] replied, "If they won't listen to Moses and the Prophets, they won't be persuaded even if somebody rises from the dead.

And, of course, Abraham was exactly right—many did not believe when Jesus did just that!

---

1   That is, with the Old Testament Scriptures.

2   To be "broken" would seem to mean to be successfully challenged so as to break down what is said. That the Bible cannot be successfully challenged so as to be *refuted*, is what He had in mind. It was the final authority. Indeed, Jesus treats His quotation of Psalm 82 as if there was nothing more that needed to be said. Some would call this "proof-texting." So be it, if Jesus thought it right to do so.

3   An expression used by the Jews to refer to the entire Old Testament.

Of great significance is the import of what Abraham said. He was affirming the ultimate authority of the Bible. If it was rejected, there was nothing more to say. It was the final authority. Even the experience of a miraculous resurrection would not measure up to that. The Bible was the authority of authorities.[4] Peter, similarly, explained that written prophecy was a "more sure word" than his unique experience on the Mount of Transfiguration (2 Peter 2:19). How much experience-oriented persons today could learn from Peter!

On the day of Pentecost, when the Spirit descended on the infant church, it was not to what had taken place alone that Peter appealed. Indeed, he backs up all that he says by quoting Joel 2 as the final authority for his explanation of the event: "this is what the prophet Joel spoke about" (Acts 2:16). The signs and wonders that had occurred, and would continue to occur during the last days that extended from the ministry of Christ until the destruction of Jerusalem in 70 AD, were themselves no final authority. They had to be authenticated and distinguished from other supposed miracles by God's authoritative Word.[5] Peter himself, though authorized to preach in the Name of Christ, was not the final Word. He did not think that people should accept what he said on his own word; rather, he considered it necessary to appeal to the Scriptures as the ultimate authority. And, in this regard, the Bereans' searching of the Scriptures to see whether what Paul said was true was commended by Luke (cf. Acts 17:11).

All in all, it seems apparent that in the Bible itself we have warrant for saying that the Scriptures are to be the final authority. The church may not take the place of the Bible. Churches and councils of men have erred. While what they say should be given due consideration, their declarations must be evaluated according to how well they accord with the Scriptures. The Scriptures, then, function as what they are everywhere called "the Word of God." They are as much His holy[6] Word as if He

---

4 See also Deuteronomy 13:1–5 where a prophetic message must be compared with the known biblical understanding about God in order to test the validity of what he says. Doctrine supersedes even seemingly fulfilled signs and wonders!

5 For more on this, see my *Signs and Wonders in the Last Days.*

6 Unique; set apart from all other books.

were to speak it audibly from heaven. Contrary to those who claim that God alone has authority and that the Scriptures do not, we may assuredly assert that between what God said verbally and what He caused to be written in the Bible, there is no difference whatsoever. God alone does have authority, but it is His prerogative to authoritatively reveal His will to His church in written form.

CHAPTER 9

MORE ABOUT THE BIBLE

W E have seen that the Scriptures are authoritative. But what does that mean to the church and those who minister in it? Simply put, an authoritative Bible is necessary for ministry. It is no good for apostles or elders to have authority if there is no authoritative standard by which to judge their teaching and action. Apart from a divinely given standard, they might be asserting their autonomous thoughts and ideas. And that is precisely what has happened where the Bible has been eliminated as the authoritative Word from God.

Such a standard must both set forth the duties of each authority figure and define the limits of his authority. Otherwise, the man himself becomes the standard. That is the problem, for instance, with legalists. The best-known legalists are the Pharisees, who lived in Palestine in New Testament times. In order to keep people from violating the commandments of God, they built a fence of their own commandments around the law. This evolved into what Jesus called the "tradition of the elders." This tradition had so covered up the Scriptures that they were virtually smothered by it. Jesus accused the Pharisees of annulling "God's Word for the sake of [their] tradition" (Matthew 15:6).

In that statement, Jesus put His finger on the pulse of the issue. Whenever anything is added to the authoritative, sufficient written Word of God, it eventually takes precedence over the Word. That is just as true of the legalists in our day who compose lists of dos and don'ts that are not found in Scripture. Sooner or later (usually sooner), these additions shape how the legalists read the Bible. Indeed, these items on the legalist's list are for all intents and purposes his Scripture. They certainly do become the authoritative standard for his faith and life – the very thing that the Bible was intended to be. There are Pharisees in our day as well as in the time of Christ.

The answer to all legalism is found in Paul's insightful statement: "that you may learn from us not to go beyond what is written" (1 Corinthians 4:6).[1] How important it is to reiterate that truth over and over again in all sorts of contexts. As Paul said, this is something that many (not only the Corinthians) need to learn.[2] People seem not to learn this on their own, so it is necessary for those who are concerned about the blight of legalism today to teach about the prohibition to "go beyond what is written." That is, they must not go beyond the good deposit of the faith. Moreover, wherever legalism persists, it should be confronted and put down. Otherwise, as we saw in the case of the Pharisees, the ideas of men will quickly take over and become the final authority, rather than the Bible.

The heart of the issue is this: Is the Bible a *sufficient* authority for faith and practice or not? The question in evangelical circles today is not so much the inspiration of the Bible, but its sufficiency. Those who wish to supplement it with psychology, by marketing strategies and the like, reveal their faulty view of the divine Authority that God has so graciously given His church. Jesus said, "But when the Spirit of truth comes, He will guide you into all truth" (John 16:13). And He also put it this way: "The Holy Spirit that the Father will send in My name, He is the One Who will teach you everything and remind you of everything that I told you" (John 14:26). These two statements clearly say that the Spirit would give the apostles *everything* they needed to carry on their work. Did the Spirit do this or not? And the second statement indicates that what Jesus was referring to was *how* the Spirit would inspire them to write the New Testament books. How is that so? When He spoke of reminding them of "everything that He told them," doubtless He was thinking of the need for supernaturally guided memories in order to write the Gospels. To write accurately, they needed to be able to remember all that Jesus did and said. Peter also spoke about sufficiency when he wrote that "His divine power has given us everything for life and godliness" (2 Peter 1:3). So

---

1   See also II John 8, 9. For a discussion of the II John passage see my book *The Use of the Rod and the Staff: A Neglected Aspect of Biblical Shepherding*.
2   The word for "learn" is *manthano*, which usually means "to learn by inquiry." But not every Christian inquires about the important issues. That is why they need instruction.

the issue is drawn – either the Scriptures are sufficient or they are not.[3] Where do you stand on this matter?

There can be only one authoritative standard of faith and practice. The biblical Christian chooses the Bible as His one and only final standard; the legalist chooses the Bible and something else (which, as we have noted, in time will take the place of the Scriptures). That is the large issue that many need to face today. Have you dealt with this question?

---

3 See also my thorough discussion of II Timothy 3:17 in *How to Help People Change.*

CHAPTER 10

THE SCRIPTURES HAVE *DUNAMIS*

A T the beginning of this book, I distinguished between *exousia* and *dunamis*. Because I have been speaking largely about *exousia* and not dunamis, it might be good to briefly review the distinction between the two. You will recall that the former is *conferred* authority, a right granted to one person by another. Jesus (as the God-man), the apostles, and the duly ordained elders of the church all possess *exousia*.[1] On the other hand, *dunamis* is what the 500-pound gorilla has: internal power to influence others. While one may have been granted *exousia*, the same person may possess only a limited amount of *dunamis*. Jesus had, to the full, both external and internal authority, each in perfect harmony with the other.

It is interesting to note that the Bible itself is said to have *dunamis*. Let's begin by looking briefly at several verses. First, Hebrews 4:12-13:

> *God's Word is alive and active, sharper than any two-edged sword, penetrating deeply enough to cut open soul and spirit and joints and marrow*[2]*; it can judge the desires and thoughts of the heart. Before Him no creature can hide, but all are naked and laid open to the eyes of Him to Whom we must give an account.*

That is *dunamis*! Scripture actively works in the lives of those whom God changes.

Clearly, the writer of the book of Hebrews taught that the Bible, which is the written Word of God, has the power to reach into the hearts of men. He speaks of it as being "active" and as "alive." It exposes and convicts people of their sin. Peter taught that it was by God's Word that

---

1   Which ultimately was conferred by God the Father.
2   Not divide between, as some think. Rather, the sword slices each open (literally, "divides *of*") to expose what lies within.

the "heavens existed and an earth was formed out of water" (2 Peter 3:5). God *spoke* and there was light! Moreover, the Word is capable of "building up" believers (Acts 20:12). And that same Word is "at work" in those who "believe" (2 Thessalonians 13). All of these verses clearly demonstrate the *dunamis* that God's Word possesses.[3]

The Word's *dunamis*, however, does not transform people automatically. It is hidden to the eyes and the ears of the "natural man" who looks upon it as "foolishness" (1 Corinthians 2:9). And even in the case of those who *have* believed, but since that time have drifted from Scripture, it is necessary for them to resume their interest in the Scriptures and to continue studying and applying them in order to become "experienced" in discernment and grow spiritually. Otherwise, one becomes "dull" and loses his grasp even on the knowledge that he once possessed and reverts to spiritual infancy (Hebrews 5:12-14). To be positively affected by God's Word, then, one must be regenerate, come to it in faith,[4] and then be enlightened by the Spirit to understand it.[5]

We read how the disciples on the road to Emmaus were positively affected when Jesus "opened their minds" and then "opened the Scriptures" to them:

> *So beginning with Moses, He went through all the prophets and explained to them in all the Scriptures the things that concerned Himself ... Then He opened their minds to understand the Scriptures ... And they said to one another, "Didn't our hearts burn within us as He spoke to us on the road, as He opened the Scriptures to us?"* (Luke 24:27, 45, 32)

The power is there to transform people, and that power is released upon regeneration and the study and application of the Word by the power of the Spirit.

---

3   I shall not mention the many ways that Psalm 119 demonstrates the power of the Scriptures to affect people. For details, see *Counsel from Psalm 119*.

4   Hebrews 4:2; 11:6.

5   According to I Corinthians 2:9–16, no one is able to appreciate and appropriate the "teachings of God's Spirit" unless he has received and possesses the Spirit.

The power of the Word of God is manifest from the very beginning of the Christian life. For instance, in Romans 1:16, we read of the gospel as the "power of God" that leads to salvation. But the gospel is a *message*, good *news*. Such news, mixed with faith (as we have seen), leads to salvation. Faith *in the message* justifies. Also, we read that "In Him you too, by hearing the Word of truth—the good news of your salvation—when you also believed in Him, were sealed with the promised Holy Spirit." That "implanted Word," when welcomed, James says, "is able to save your souls" (James 1:21). Moreover, the Scriptures used by that Spirit give hope to the justified believer (Romans 15:4, 13). In verse 13, the Spirit is said to produce hope. In verse 4, we see that He does this not apart from but through the Scriptures. It is by the Word, which is "the Spirit's sword,"[6] that we are able to fight the battles of the Christian life successfully (Ephesians 6:17). And it must be remembered, when God sends forth His Word, it never returns to Him void, but accomplishes precisely what He intends it to accomplish (Isaiah 55:11).

In all of these passages, it is not difficult to discern something of the *dunamis* of the Word of God. Just notice the operative verbs that speak of what the Word *does*. Yet the Word does not work alone; both the Spirit and the person who is affected contribute to its effectiveness. It is the Spirit and the Word that are at work initially to transform the person; then, following regeneration, it is the Spirit and the believer who becomes a "doer of the Word" (and not a "hearer only") who together bring about growth (James 1:22).

So it is of great importance for every believer who serves Jesus Christ to recognize that the power that He needs to back up and reinforce his *exousia* comes from the Word of God, which itself has *dunamis*. And as the Christian believes, appropriates, and practices, the Word adds power to his conferred authority. The importance of the written Word of power must not be minimized. When it is minimized or compromised, those who sit under weakened ministries are likely to have only "a form of godliness" while "rejecting its power" (2 Timothy 3:5).

---

6   It is said to be *His* sword because He forged and uses it as such.

CHAPTER 11

TEACH WITH AUTHORITY

THE proper biblical exercise of authority in Christ's church involves several factors (which I will deal with in this chapter and chapters 12–13). The first is teaching with authority. Paul wrote to Titus, "Speak these things; urge and convict, with recognition that you have full authority to give orders. Let nobody disregard you" (Titus 3:15). That is a comprehensive command that we must unpack and apply in this and the next two chapters.

Almost every form of ministry involves teaching, whether it be preaching, counseling, guidance, instruction, or whatever. In *Teaching to Observe,* I note the importance of teaching in biblical counseling, and I show that the Lord does not consider teaching as cramming facts into one's head, only to be regurgitated at some later time. Instead, He identifies teaching as applying His truth to people's lives so that they can better glorify Him. The command in Matthew 28:20, from which the title of the book came, reads this way: "[teach] them to observe all that I have commanded you." The passage indicates that those who are discipled to Christ must be taught to engage in commandment-oriented living rather than the feeling-oriented living that is so common today.

More than merely telling us to teach in this way, Jesus Himself became the model for all the teaching that we do. His teaching, as we have observed earlier, led people to exclaim over the difference between His teaching and the scribes' (the religious teachers of the day). How was that? We read that His listeners were "astonished at His teaching, because He taught them *as an authority*, and not as the scribes" (Mark 1:22, emphasis mine). That same fact ought to be the hallmark of the biblical teacher. Because he has an authoritative Book from God, it is possible for him also to teach authoritatively. And it is incumbent upon him to do so.

Of course, no teacher today is inspired or inerrant, even with the inspired Scriptures as his guide. Teachers may misinterpret, fail to comprehend, and so on. But the teacher who knows his Bible has every reason to speak with authority when he thoroughly understands the Scriptures.

Indeed, this is a hallmark of truly biblical counseling. It ought always be said that those who counsel in God's Name give clear, straight, biblical answers (cf. Colossians 4:4). They do not hedge or provide fuzzy ideas. Now, that does not mean that every counselor has answers to every problem. But it does mean that he will honestly tell a counselee when he does not know rather than try to bluff his way through a counseling session. He will speak authoritatively only upon those matters about which he is certain.

The same is true about other teaching. I do not preach about "baptism for the dead" mentioned in 1 Corinthians 15:29 because I simply do not understand what Paul was referring to. I once read over thirty explanations of the passage in a journal, and every one of them convinced me until I read the next! I have always made it a policy that if I could not speak authoritatively about a matter from the Scriptures, I would not preach about that matter until I could. That is because people do not need to hear about my guesses, suppositions, suggestions, or surmises. What they need is the infallible Word of the living God presented authoritatively. Whenever someone speaks for the Lord, he should speak in a way that His Lord did and in the manner that His Word does—both of which presented truth with authority. He must not dilute that authority by some weak presentation.

Unless truth, which should be taught for the sake of life, as we saw (cf. Titus 1:1), is accurate, clear, and direct, people will not know how to live. That is one of the reasons why the church, though rich in numbers and wealth, is so poor in sturdy saints! All teachers ought to keep this in mind. It is their task to "root and ground believers in their faith" (Ephesians 3:17). That will happen when teaching itself is so solidly rooted and grounded that it can only be presented authoritatively.

Many pastors, however, came through seminaries where much speculative material was presented in theoretical, abstract form. It has been so long since they have heard truth presented authoritatively, in a form adapted to everyday living, that they do not know how to do it. Their professors so qualified every statement they made that they may have picked up that habit from them. Consequently, their congregations are served a dish every Sunday that is hard to identify as fish or fowl. Moreover, the form in which they receive it makes it indigestible. It is time that Christian teachers of every sort learn from Jesus, Who used simple language and illustrative materials, and Who told His listeners exactly what He meant in words that had the ring of certainty.

Sometimes people think it is only the hard truths that must be presented with authority. Surely, they must be—even when it is difficult for listeners to hear them. But it is also the glorious truths of our wonderful salvation that must be presented this way also. No teacher has a right to present the way of salvation in a manner that leaves his listeners with doubts. No teacher should fudge his teaching, or trim his sails, for the sake of one or two among his listeners who might be angered by what the Bible teaches. He must teach the "whole counsel of God" with all of the authority that is found in the Bible itself.

God's authoritative truth, found in His authoritative Word, must be proclaimed authoritatively by one who has been granted God's authority. How authoritative is your teaching?

CHAPTER 12

EXHORT AUTHORITATIVELY

THE second fact that may be derived from Titus 3:15 is that those who teach in God's Name must *exhort* authoritatively. Paul said,

> *Urge and convict with recognition that you have full authority to give orders.*

Urging and convicting have to do with applying the Word of God to the lives of the listeners to bring about the change that God requires of them. In other words, people must be *exhorted* from Scripture to hear and do what God says.

Commenting on 2 Timothy 4:2, in which Paul urged Timothy to "reprove, rebuke, exhort," Calvin wrote, "By these words he means that we have need of many excitements to urge us to advance in the right course." And he stresses the need for "increased vehemence and threatenings whenever necessary."[1]

This exhortation, like the teaching with which it is coupled (exhortation must grow out of teaching and may not properly be divorced from it[2]), is so authoritative that Paul insisted Titus must not allow anyone to disregard it. One may bristle under it, he may challenge it, he may get angry about it, but he must not be allowed to disregard it so that it has no effect on him, either positively or negatively.

Certainly, much of the preaching and teaching that is done today elicits very little response from listeners. Relatively few changes occur; most listeners are neither angered nor disturbed. Few are convicted of their sinful lifestyles enough to cry out for help.[3] Probably that is because, in

---

1   New Testament Commentary, Volume 21, p. 258.
2   Calvin also wrote, "Both exhortation and reproofs are merely aids to doctrine and, therefore, have little weight without it." Ibid.
3   See my book *How to Help People Change* for an explanation of conviction.

most cases, there is so little exhortation or because what one hears isn't authoritative. Surely there is a place in teaching for demanding change in the Name of the Lord. Yet, sadly, in some seminaries today, preachers are taught a form of biblical-theological preaching that debases application and exhortation. Such teachers, and the preachers who follow these dictums, should reread this strong word from Paul to Titus.

The word "urge" (or "persuade"), which is used here, is *parakaleo*. This term is broad in scope and refers to doing whatever one finds necessary to bring about a needed result. Of course, the range of possibilities upon which one may draw is prescribed by the Bible. The word in this context clearly pertains to the use of exhortation.

A large part of successful biblical counseling and preaching has to do with seeing that the listener not only understands, but that he also *responds* to what he is taught. A caring, effective teacher is concerned to do this *in order to change* the thinking and living of his students. That is what Paul had in mind when he told Titus not to allow anyone to "disregard" him; he was thinking of the benefit of his listeners.

People today are experts at disregarding what they hear. They let truth – God's truth – go in one ear and out the other. Many listeners have become adept at hearing in such a way that truth is stored for use with others ("Joe needs to hear this!") or for some future date when they may need to do something about the matter ("someday I may need to do this"). These are but a few of the dozens of ways people learn to disregard truth.

But good teachers do not allow this to happen. They challenge the listener to heed God's Word. In order to make a difference in the way that truth is received, a number of possible measures may have to be taken. Principal among these is the use of strong exhortation. The matter may have to be addressed directly in an authoritative manner. Obviously, Paul (perhaps to the consternation of those who were looking over Titus' shoulder as he read Paul's letter) instructed Titus to use *full authority* and even issue *orders* to those who continued to disregard God's truth. After all, it was neither Paul's nor Titus' teaching, but rather God's, that they were avoiding. But God may not be disregarded with impunity.

It may be that the teacher is dull and uninteresting as well as unauthoritative. If these are the problems, then he must correct his manner of teaching or, if he doesn't know how to, get help. He may not misrepresent God's exciting Word by his poor, dull explanation and presentation.

And it may be that the listener hears God's truth and wants to follow it, but receives absolutely no instruction about how to put it into practice in his daily living. If the teacher knows truth only abstractly, he will not be able to help his congregation very much. He must know what it means to translate truth into day-by-day living. He must understand his listeners' difficulties and struggles. He needs to be able to offer "how-to" advice that grows out of and is consistent with the Bible at every point. The "what to" is every bit as essential as the "how to." There is no question about how Jesus taught: He accompanied the "what" with the "how."[4]

To be effective, exhortation must be given authoritatively and must not be disregarded. That is the bottom line of what Paul said. Preacher, how significant is this matter to you when you preach?

---

4   See the Sermon on the Mount, where Jesus again and again tells his listeners what to do and then explains how not to do it, followed by instructions about how to do it properly.

Chapter 13

Use Authority Fully

Paul concludes his letter to Titus by saying that he should speak and exhort "with all authority." That phrase means "with (full or complete) authority." But how far does "full authority" extend? Did those words give Titus—and elders of the church today—the right to order people around according to their own whims? The words, on the face of them, seem to grant unlimited authority. If true, that might easily turn into tyranny.

The concept of "full authority" must be understood in context. Presumably, there were those who were attempting to "disregard" what Titus taught. This tendency to "think around" him (as the Greek word translated "disregard" means) had to be countered. Paul was saying that Titus should not allow this situation to continue. Rather, he had full authority to order those who failed to listen to his teaching to heed it. This order, if not obeyed, might have to be followed by the exercise of church discipline. Christian teachers may not be as frank as a teacher at Johns Hopkins University who told us, "I don't care whether you get this material or not. All I have to do is to present it!" But sometimes their presentations make you wonder. Biblical teaching involves not only imparting information, but also seeing to it that it is presented in such a way that anyone with a willing mind will "get it." Moreover, such teaching is concerned that a student will "get it" in such a practical way that he can use it. And finally, it concerns itself with whether or not the student uses it profitably in his life.[1]

In addition to those who were failing to hear Titus' sound teaching, there were also those who were rebellious (Titus 1:10) and some who

---

1 In some churches there may be concern about the disregard that many of the members show for the truth, but nothing is done to remedy the situation. Paul expected Titus to use his God-given authority directly and definitively to deal with the matter.

were schismatic (Titus 3:10). In the light of that situation, Paul urged Titus to use to the full the authority of Christ that had been given to him. He was not granting unlimited authority, but urging Titus not to be reluctant to use the authority that he possessed to the fullest. Titus was to use as much of that authority as necessary—even up to its very limit— to quell this rebellion and put down every schismatic move.

That is the problem today. Elders, to whom Christ has given adequate authority to quash divisive words and actions, fail to use that authority. Either they do not realize that they have the authority to confront and order disruptive persons to stop their nefarious activities, or, knowing this, they simply fail to do what they know they ought. Either way, because of this appalling lack of authority in many churches, people are allowed to do just about whatever they please. All to the injury of God's flock! Because of this confusion and disruption, which is due to the failure to exercise duly granted authority, many drift away from the church. They do not want to become embroiled in turmoil and controversy. But the words of Titus 1 clearly encourage the elder to exert whatever authority that is necessary to "shut the mouths" of those who are causing trouble (Titus 1:11). In how many congregations do elders do so?

It is true that one need not always use one's authority to the full. If possible, he is to "teach the trustworthy Word" in such a way that he will "encourage" listeners in living righteously (Titus 1:9). But if they reject this teaching or gainsay it, then he must "convict of their error those who object" (Titus 1:9). This "conviction" (also mentioned in Titus 2:15) consists of making out a case from the Scriptures against an offender that, were one to press it in a law court, would bring about his conviction. The word "convict" has legal implications and was used in trying lawbreakers in court. The term has the idea of rebuke or reproof in it, but it is a rebuke that is effectively brought to bear upon an offender.

The "rebellious persons," Paul says, were "vain talkers and deceivers." Their mouths needed to be shut by sound teaching and by the exercise of the authority of Christ because they were "upsetting whole households by teaching things that they shouldn't for the sake of shameful gain" (Titus 1:11). Obviously, these persons were becoming destructive to the infant churches that Titus was to organize on the island of Crete. And that is just the time when one must take special care to put down all attempts of such persons to "take over" and get control of these churches.

It is especially important to silence any who carry on this way at the inception of a new church because, in a small group, even one or two people can have great influence for ill. The exercise of authority, then, ought to be evident from the earliest days of a new congregation. It is, however, precisely then that elders are most hesitant to use their authority. They are looking for all the new members they can get and will often put up with the most abominable disregard for God's truth just to hold on to every person possible. That is a bad bargain! In the long run, when these persons have gained influence enough "to drag away disciples to follow them" (Acts 20:30), they will cause even greater disturbance and, in the end, the church will lose more members than if it had rejected the "vain talkers" at the beginning (Titus 3:10). Never put off dealing with divisive persons.

The exercise of authority must not be arbitrary, and it must not be used unless all teaching, exhortation, and persuasion fail. But Christ gave authority to the officers of His church to *use*. And use it they must when necessary, or they will not be good shepherds of the flock. Full use of authority in many cases would mean the use of church discipline in which, because of their contumacy, some are put out of the church. The "old leaven" is cleaned out of the church for three reasons: the honor of God's Name, the welfare of the church, and the repentance of the offender. Those who repent after exclusion from the congregation must be readmitted to their full status as members in love, forgiven by the church, and given all the assistance necessary to make a good transition back into the fellowship of God's people (2 Corinthians 2:6-8). For help in how to discipline in a scriptural manner, see my book *The Handbook of Church Discipline.*

Full authority also comprises a couple of other factors. It means that one may not use authority with reference to only *some* issues while avoiding others. For instance, schismatics must not be subject to discipline while gossips are not. Indeed, in some cases, gossip may lead to even more damage and division than attempted schism. Both ought to be dealt with using the full authority of which the Bible speaks. There is a tendency to avoid certain sins in the congregation while coming down too hard on others. Full use of authority, on the contrary, means to avoid none and to treat all according to the way in which the Bible directs.

Using authority to its full extent would also include exercising authority with respect to *all* persons alike. There must be no fear or favor given. Rich persons as well as poor must be treated alike. Not only ought younger men and women be urged to subject themselves to the leadership of the church, but older ones as well (Titus 2:1-8). There is a tendency to allow certain factors to influence elders in ways that are not appropriate. James speaks strongly against favoritism (James 2:1-7). To those who fall prey to this vice, he directs this question: "Haven't you discriminated among yourselves and become judges with evil thoughts?" (James 2:4). Here, James is getting at the motives involved. He asks the perpetrator to examine himself to see whether or not he is acting out of evil motives.[2] It is not our task to make judgments that distinguish who we will use discipline on and who we will not on any basis other than that which the Bible sets forth: contumacy (the unwillingness to submit to the properly exercised authority of Christ).

In all of this, the elder must avoid a tendency to be rough, harsh, and demanding. Authority must always be shown as a loving, helpful thing. Paul put it this way:

> *Remind them … to insult nobody, not to be quarrelsome; to be gentle, demonstrating full consideration for every person. At one time we too were foolish, disobedient, deceived, and enslaved to various desires and pleasures, going along through life with malice and envy, hated by others and hating them* (Titus 3:1-3).

What a check to the possible abuse of authority! In order not to fall into the trap of a harsh, unfeeling use of this important tool for maintaining order in the church, Paul asks those in authority to remember

---

2   Notice, James does not judge another's heart, but calls upon the one whose behavior may indicate "evil thoughts" to look into his heart himself. Many today speak and write unbiblically as if they were able to know what is in another's heart.

their own past. Before the grace of God was showered upon us in "deep affection" as it was "poured out effusively through Jesus Christ" (Titus 3:4, 6), all of us went our own willful ways. And it was only by this tender mercy shown to us by God in His Son that we were "justified by His grace" and became "heirs to the hope of eternal life" (Titus 3:7). Remembering this, in the full exercise of authority, we should "give orders" that are but a reiteration of the commandments of Christ (Matthew 28:20) in such a way that, as we deal with people, we give them no reason to reject God's good Word because of our misuse and abuse of authority. Rather, "in every way" we are to "make the teaching of God our Savior inviting" (Titus 2:10).

I have spent a good bit of time setting forth information about authority from the book of Titus. That is because this book deals with the matter so fully. Since there is no opportunity in this volume to look into every aspect of the use of authority in Titus, I encourage you to read through the book, keeping in mind that Paul is very concerned with the proper use of authority. Learn and apply what you read.

CHAPTER 14
BE BOLD

ONE of the major reasons for the authority drain is fear. Elders, and many of their people, are simply afraid of what the exercise of authority may do. They fear losing members, retaliation, what others might say or think of them, and so on. Some, more wisely, fear that they may do something wrong.

The word "boldness" (*parrasia*) is a key word in the book of Acts. From the beginning to the end, it appears again and again as a characteristic of the apostles who preached the gospel from Jerusalem to Rome. What does this word mean? There are two words for "boldness" in the New Testament Scriptures. The first means "daring activity." That is not the term that we are considering. *Parresia*, the second word, means "speaking, unencumbered by fear of consequences." This sort of boldness is what every elder needs. There is nothing to fear when authority is used, as God directs, to say and do what Scripture requires. God will bless those who follow His Word and preserve them and the church that they serve.

That is not to say that there will not be trouble as the result of asserting Christ's authority. People will react. They may object. They could possibly slander. But as I said, there is nothing to fear if authority is asserted biblically. Why not? Because I repeat, God will bless us when we follow His instructions. And authority, rightly exercised, does not *create* problems. It merely exposes already existing problems. The church needs officers who are willing to confront, to speak authoritatively, unencumbered by fear of consequences.

Remember, authority is not some passive possession of power to be used only when the elders serve the Lord's Supper. No. *Epitage*, mentioned in Titus 2:15, is a commanding, ordering authority. It is one that, if not heeded, warns about the possibility of also using the elder's binding and loosing authority. And further, when that warning is disregarded, it is an authority that proceeds to the process of church discipline.

Boldness (*parresia*) is a quality that God gives; it is not one that is native to sinners. Even the apostles prayed for boldness, saying, "So now, Lord, take note of their threats and give Your slaves all the boldness needed to speak Your Word" (Acts 4:29). And Paul, whom we rightly consider a brave man, urged the Ephesians to "pray... that I may speak boldly, as indeed I should" (Ephesians 6:19, 20). If elders want to become the right sort of elders, speaking boldly with Christ's authority, they should ask God to work boldness in them as they read the Scriptures and seek to implement what they read when authority is needed. It should help to recognize that even the apostle Paul had problems with exerting authority and had to ask churches to pray that he would be bold enough to do so. If he needed to ask, so do you.

Boldness is not crudeness. Nor is it brashness. It is certainly not the assertion of one's own opinions or insisting on his own way. It is a matter of bringing the truth of God's Word to bear on a situation in which people are not obeying it. Always, that boldness must come from a proper assurance that one has interpreted God's Word as he should. Boldness will always diminish in proportion to one's uncertainty about his correct interpretation of a text. A preacher or ruling elder must be able to say, "Thus says the Lord," with a confidence that is born out of careful exegesis. So another reason for the lack of boldness in asserting authority is uncertainty. Doubtless, many refuse to speak with authority because they are not sure enough about what they have to say. They are correct in not speaking authoritatively under those circumstances. But they are not right in allowing the situation to persist. If they do not understand the Scriptures adequately enough to make definite statements about matters of discipline and so on, they should take the time and make the effort to learn the answers that they need. There is no excuse for elders either not knowing what to do as elders or not caring enough to find out.

If you are not as bold in what you do and say as an elder, what is your problem? Is it fear? Is it a lack of concern? Is it failure to discover the answers to questions due to a lack of effort on your part? What is it? Whatever the problem, it is your obligation to pinpoint it and remedy it. Ask God to help you learn what it is—and to help you to become bold!

CHAPTER 15

SUBMISSION—THE OTHER SIDE OF THE EQUATION

I would be remiss to speak of authority and not discuss the relationship of those who are under that authority. Authority means nothing if there are no individuals over whom one has authority, those who acknowledge that authority and submit to it. In such a relationship, there is one who *yields* and one who *wields* authority. Accordingly, when the Bible speaks of authority, it also implies *submission*.

Paul introduces the matter of authority and submission in this way: "Submit yourselves to one another out of respect for Christ" (Ephesians 5:21). He proceeds in chapters five and six to discuss three applications: the submission of wives to their own husbands, the submission of children to their parents, and the submission of slaves to their masters. In each of these relationships, what Paul has in view is the way in which *Christian* wives, children, and slaves are to submit to one in authority.[1]

But what does "submission" mean? What does it require of the one who is to submit? The word *upotasso* is a military term that means to subordinate oneself to another of higher rank. In the Scriptures, it has to do with the role one has in a given context in relationship to other persons. It has nothing directly to do with *dunamis*. One may have much greater inner authority (*dunamis*) than another, while at the same time standing in a lesser *exousia* relationship to him. The person with the uniform may not possess as much *dunamis* as the one over whom he exercises *exousia*. While that is not the ideal situation in the church, in a world where all is not perfect, one may often encounter it.

---

1 Some, quite erroneously, take verse 21 to say that all Christians, regardless of their role and their authority, must submit to one another. If correct, that understanding of the verse would, of course, destroy the authority/submissions relationships Paul was about to discuss. No one would have authority over another since everyone would be required to submit to everyone else. Even a little thought should convince those who are anxious to break down the authority of husbands over wives that this rather silly attempt is futile.

Submission, as we are dealing with it in this chapter, then, has largely to do with *exousia*.

To submit oneself to an officer of the church means to recognize that God has granted authority to the church, and that authority must be obeyed. It is not another person's *dunamis* to which he submits, but to his God-given *exousia*. Therefore, we are dealing specifically with elders, who are appointed to the only office that carries church authority. They are ordained (set apart, appointed) to the work of "managing" (*proistemi*) the body of people gathered together to constitute a church in a given area. Paul wrote:

> *Now we ask you, brothers, to recognize those who labor among you, and* **manage** *you in the Lord, and counsel you. Think quite highly of them in love because of their work. Be at peace among yourselves* (1 Thessalonians 5:12, 13; emphasis mine).

This "managing" task is the primary concern for elders. In writing to Timothy, Paul spoke of "the elders who *manage* well" receiving "double pay."[2] He also mentioned those who, in addition to managing, also preached and taught. All elders manage as the fundamental task assigned to them, but some also carry out the two additional functions of preaching and teaching. Thus, the eldership is one office, embracing two functions.

It is in the fundamental managing function that the elder's authority basically exists; here is what the writer of Hebrews had to say:

> *Obey your leaders and submit to them. They are keeping watch over your lives as men who will have to give an account. Obey so that they may do this with joy and not as a burden, since that wouldn't be to your advantage* (Hebrews 13:17).

---

2 That Paul referred to double pay, not honor (as the King James Version wrongly translated the Greek word *time*) is plain from the Old Testament verses that are quoted in the next verse (v. 18) which speak of not muzzling the ox and paying a worker the wages he has earned. One wonders what it was that induced the translators to err when the correct translation was so obvious.

There is no doubt, then, that the office of elder carried authority. When an elder functioned as a "manager" who "kept watch" over the flock, from time to time he would find it necessary to issue orders (not always in a formal way, of course) that should be "obeyed." Again, in this passage, the reader is told to "submit" to him because of this authority. It is this requirement of submission that turns off so many today.

There is a sinful built-in bias against authority, as I noted earlier, which causes many to bristle when someone speaks of "submitting" and "obeying." This bias is often found even in Christians. But it is a bias that they must overcome. While it is important to call upon elders to recognize and use their God-given authority according to the biblical principles that govern it, it is every bit as important to call upon members to acknowledge that their authority is from God and to submit to it!

When facing the prospect of submitting to an elder, a Christian must immediately check the feelings that may arise from his inner tendency to rebel. He should not say or think, "Who is Joe to tell me what to do or not to do?" If he does, he has a problem with submission and must deal with it. Submission does not come easily to those who, from birth, have had the desire to be autonomous. But a person can begin to develop a new attitude if he will only recognize that, ultimately, it is not to the elder himself that he submits, but to the Lord in Whose Name the elder speaks.

Once more, reader (especially if you are struggling with the idea of submission right now), remember that you do not ask the policeman whether he is a good husband and father before you are willing to receive a ticket from him. You remember that he functions as an arm of the state, acting under its authority. And, moreover, you remember that this authority ultimately comes from God. So to submit to the policeman—or to the elder—is to submit to God.

"I know it says so, but how come I have to submit to him? He's only another member of the church, just as I am."

Before going further, let me remind you of Korah's rebellion in which he and others were saying much the same thing. They, too, called *all* the people "holy," as if they all had the same authority. But the very word "holy" means that something is set apart from others similar to it for a special purpose. That is exactly what calling men to take upon themselves the work of the elder is all about: it is the setting apart of some qualified men for the special purposes of "managing," and "preaching and teaching." Every organization—including the church—must have leaders and must grant them authority to lead.

"Well, yes. I know intellectually that this must be so. The verses that you have cited unmistakably teach what you are saying, but there is still something that doesn't seem right about 'submitting' to someone who lives down the street from me!"

If the policeman we've used as an example lived down the street, would you still need to submit to him if he were to give you a ticket?

"Yeah. I guess so. But if I knew him well, as a friend, then it would be easier. I know that if he had to do so but didn't want to since he was a friend, I could take it better."

Ah! I think I have found one of the difficulties that you are facing. You don't look on your elders as friends. I am not sure what the reason for this is, but from your side of the relationship, at least, it is your obligation to become friendly with them. Remember the passage in 1 Thessalonians 5:12-13? There it says "recognize" your elders. That word, literally, is "know" them. It is your task to get to know your elders. And when you do, you must look for those things that, as Paul urges, will make you "think quite highly of them." You see, if you maintain a stand-offish attitude, you may only see them as "authoritarian" rather than as those who properly exercise authority in God's Name for your benefit.

"Okay. That helps a bit. But shouldn't they act in a friendly manner to me as well? Is this all a one-way street?"

Of course they should. In John 10, Jesus sets forth the relationship of sheep to a good shepherd. What He mentions there is that the sheep know the shepherd and his voice. And He also says that a good shepherd loves the sheep and knows each by name. In other words, there is such a close bond between them that you could describe it as nothing less than a close friendship.

"Well, I think that if I had that sort of relationship with the elders in my church, it would make a difference. You are probably right."

Certainly, I believe it would. Now, when an elder helps out a member of the flock in time of need, that goes a long way toward cementing a warm bond between them. Perhaps one of the problems is that elders do not function in the pastoral role that is everywhere designated as a primary duty of elders (cf. Acts 20, 1 Peter 5).

"Now you may have put your finger on it. If I saw more of my elders in a personal way, ministering to me and to other members of the flock—and even just getting to know them as friends – that surely would make a difference."

Good. Why not call upon your elder when you need help? That might be a beginning toward developing the warm relationship that you read about in John 10. And, in addition, why not invite him and his wife to dinner?

So you begin to see, don't you, that your struggle with submission may stem at least in part from your failure to make friends with your elders, and from your failing to call upon them in time of need. Turning that around, by beginning to remedy this lack, should begin to quell the struggle. Too many Christians allow their remaining sinful bias against authority to grow and dominate their view of the elder. Under those conditions, he doesn't stand a chance of helping as he was intended to.

Granted, many elders need to become better acquainted with the members of the flock. From their side of the relationship, that too needs improvement. And rather than merely attend meetings and debate and vote, elders need to be out among the members of the flock, lending help to needy sheep. And they must get to know them individually. When they do, they will be of greater benefit to them, and their members will be more inclined to submit whenever necessary.

Submission involves two things: *obedience*, when called for on biblical grounds, and *respect* (the word used in Ephesians 5:21). When one respects Christ's authority, he also respects Jesus Christ Himself. The word "respect" in the original is "fear." While it largely has the idea of respect, respect itself never completely loses the notion of fear.[3] To "obey your leaders" is simply to do as they say—whenever they require you to do something clearly biblical.

---

3   The same is true of the English word "respect." If you were to ask a zoo keeper about our 500-pound gorilla, he would be likely to say, "I respect him; I'd be a fool to take him for granted." The note of "fear" lingers behind that use of the word respect.

"What if they don't? What if they ask me to do something that is out of accord with the Bible?"

The apostles themselves settled this matter when dealing with the problem of orders that conflicted with biblical imperatives. They said, "We must obey God rather than men" (Acts 5:29). Since God never gave anyone authority to command another to disobey His Word, any such command issues from "men" and not from "God." But while out of conscience toward God, a person must refuse to obey any order that conflicts with Scripture, he must disagree in a respectful manner, citing the pertinent scripture passages that lead to his refusal, and explaining his interpretation of them.

So submission to the elders of the church is certainly needed. And so far as possible, both elders and members must create the conditions under which submission will come easily.

CHAPTER 16

LIMITS TO THE CHURCH'S AUTHORITY

THERE is no question that church authority is limited.[1] God did not, for instance, give the church the authority to send people to jail, to put others to death, or to fight wars. Jesus made this perfectly clear when he told Pilate that His kingdom is:

> ...not from this world. If My kingdom were from this world, My servants would have fought to keep Me from being delivered to the Jews. But the fact is, My kingdom isn't from here (John 18:36).

It is plain, then, that the authority of the church, though very powerful, does not extend into the governmental arena. It is its own spiritual kingdom, with its own government. "It is not from here," Jesus explained. The church was not organized from among men or by them as a product of this world. Rather, it was founded by God Himself, and because its source is heavenly, the church is appropriately called "the Kingdom of God" and "the Kingdom of Heaven." These two titles refer to the very same entity, as many have clearly shown, and designate both the *Person* from Whom the kingdom comes and the *place* from which it comes. Neither the place nor the Person are earthly. So in contrasting the two governments, we see the error of wanting to extend the church's authority to earthly governments.

Neither does the church have the authority to tell people how to conduct business, nor does it have any authority to choose and command individuals to marry one another. There are, however, aspects of business and of the home about which the Bible does speak. Elders do have the obligation to forbid their members from cheating others in a business

---

[1] Here we are talking about limits to the *church's* authority, not to the authority of Christ Who has all authority in the heavens and in the earth (Matthew 28:18–20).

transaction, and to discipline them if they do not listen. They do have authority to tell anyone that they should not marry unbelievers, and, again, they may discipline them if they do. Indeed, if Christians are involved in governmental activities, they must follow Christian principles and practices in those areas, or they should be disciplined for not doing so.[2] In other words, although the church is not to be engaged in business, in running its members' homes, and the like, it does reach into those areas to make sure that broad-ranging biblical principles are faithfully followed.

So as long as a church member lives and acts properly within the area of these biblical principles, in whatever area of life he moves, he is under the watchful care of the elders of the flock. All such activity is subject to the scrutiny, biblical direction, and discipline of the church. However, apart from becoming involved in such matters and managing the daily affairs of the church itself, the elders have no authoritative jurisdiction over their members.

The limitation of church authority, then, extends to the business of the Kingdom of God as that is revealed in the Bible. Elders have no business dictating to members how or what they should do with reference to what cars they buy, how to grow flowers, or a hundred other matters for which there is no biblical direction. But as a Christian participates in any given activity conducted in some area other than within the government of the church itself, his action is subject to the authority and review by the church with respect to his attitudes, his words, and his behavior. These must all accord with the two great commandments: to love God with all one's heart, mind, and strength, and to love one's neighbor as oneself. In other words, if someone plants a tree too close to his neighbor's boundary line, knowing that his neighbor would be displeased, and the neighbor failed to elicit a remedy by persuasion, he would be perfectly justified in pressing charges against him in his congregation, and the offender would be subject to discipline. If in a business deal one Christian claims that another has cheated him, he too may bring charges against the one who allegedly did the wrong.

---

2   Bill Clinton should have been disciplined by his church for his sinful activities, but the church had no right to tell him how to conduct his normal governmental work.

When discipline is rendered in favor of the complainant, and the offender acts contumaciously (unwilling to repent), he may be punished with no greater punishment than banishment from the visible church (though that is quite serious). The church has no right to have him locked up or fined, as the church did in the Old Testament. The state must take care of those matters.

The fundamental difference between the theocracy in Israel and the church in this era is that there *was* a "worldly" side to the former administration, which is no longer true during this administration of the kingdom. In one sense, it was from this world. In the old order, which was done away with, the church and the state were intertwined so that actions taken by the church were also actions of the earthly government, and vice versa. The impact that this overall limitation of authority has upon the church is of great importance. Whenever the church and the state have become closely allied, both the church and the state have suffered.

The implications of the limitation of church authority reach to many of the movements that well-meaning but ill-informed Christians currently waste much energy, time, and money promoting. Instead, they ought to busy themselves and spend their money spreading the message of good news, shoring up themselves and other believers in their faith, and furthering those activities that have positive spiritual consequences – just as the apostles and the elders of the early church did.

I know this sounds like a retreatist mentality. It has been widely criticized by some in the church today. But it is not really so. It is the way in which the church has always properly furthered its influence for Christ in this world. Indeed, one sees Jesus gathering no group of people to support any cause other than the building of His church (Matthew 16:18). We see the apostles preaching the gospel everywhere, founding churches, and doing all that they can to regulate them and build up their members in their faith. We see them deeply concerned about the spiritual welfare of the saints and—so far as it involved the household of faith—the physical and monetary well-being of those who were suffering under persecution. But we do not see them building soup kitchens for the community or mobilizing forces to fight abortion and infanticide (both of which were legal evils in the Roman Empire). The concern was always the soul of the individual and his eternal welfare.

As I said, this approach is often called retreatist: fleeing from the world. Wrong. Did Paul flee when he traversed the Mediterranean proclaiming Christ? Certainly not. He attacked and penetrated Satan's territory and took captives for Christ. The issue is not whether to go into the world and deal with unbelievers; it is about how one does so. It is about what he does when coming into contact with them. Is he to be involved in promoting those activities of the so-called "social gospel" (which is not the gospel at all), or is he to busy himself with spreading the good news of the Kingdom to the salvation of men, women, and children everywhere? That is the main issue.

Cities and nations have been changed for good by the latter (supposedly retreatist) approach to the unbelieving world; the former has shown no such effect upon society. Why is that? Because man's heart is the problem behind all the ills in society. You can change his outward conditions, you can change his outer behavior, but if there is no change wrought in his heart by the Holy Spirit, no lasting and truly beneficial change takes place.

That surely is one reason why the limitation of authority given to the church draws a circle around her arena of spiritual warfare (cf. II Corinthians 10) in this world and refuses to give her authority to participate in that which is outside of that circle. This circle, which hems her in, when carefully observed by the church, keeps her on the track. She has enough to keep her busy in ways that are legitimate. She does not need to take on tasks that are outside the realm of her legitimate authority, tasks to which her Lord never called her. Limits, then, are of significance to every Christian.

CHAPTER 17

WOMEN IN AUTHORITY?

IN this age, it is chic to be Politically Correct, a pitfall the church has also fallen into. Feminism, in particular, has reared its head: women want to hold positions of authority in the church. The current feminist assault on the duly constituted office of elder is a fundamental attack on Christ's rightful authority over His church. Against clear biblical instruction to the contrary, both liberals and avant-garde "evangelicals"[1] claim the right to ordain women to the ministry. They have absolutely no authoritative word from the Lord allowing this. In contrast, the authoritative teaching of the Scriptures is as follows:

> *Let a woman learn in silence with complete submissiveness. I don't permit a woman to teach or exercise authority over a man but to remain silent. Adam was formed first, then Eve; and Adam was not deceived, but the woman being entirely deceived fell into transgression* (1 Timothy 2:11-14).

In this passage, notice two things:

1. The two functions of elders are once again set forth (to teach and to rule[2]), and both tasks are closed to women.
2. The reasons given by Paul are not culturally driven, as some have claimed in order to avoid the prohibition, but are based on two of the most non-cultural events that have ever occurred: creation and the fall! Even in a perfect culture Eve was deceived.

Treating the latter reason first, it should be enough to observe that the only "culture" involved was God Himself and His perfect creation.

---

1   A group to be carefully watched as the source of what may become the new liberalism.

2   See also I Timothy 5:17; Ephesians 4:11.

Like it or not, those who use lame "reasons" such as cultural conditioning should be ashamed to do so. Instead, they simply ought to admit that they don't like the prohibition and that they refuse to submit (as Paul says they should) to it as God's authoritative Word in Scripture. The liberals who agree that the Scriptures do prohibit women from assuming places of authority in the church, but say that they don't believe in the inspiration of the Bible, are more honest.

A word should be spoken about the two phrases "exercise authority over" and "be silent." The word translated "exercise authority" is *authenteo,* which means "to be the master over," or even "to domineer." Those translations make it abundantly clear that for a woman to arrogate to herself some dominant role over a man can only be considered a domineering act on her part.

"Aha!" someone says, "there is no explicit reference to her exercising *exousia,* then."

Don't be too sure. The meaning of the word reaches beyond *exousia* to the place where a woman, by assuming a place of authority in the church, does *more* than exercise authority over him; she arrogantly assumes a wrongful, domineering place by ruling over and authoritatively teaching the man. Instead of being in submission to his rule and teaching, she has taken it upon herself to steal and then step into his shoes! (He may not have been in his shoes to begin with, in which case both are sinning.) If anything, the expression is much stronger than if Paul had merely said "exercises authority." Perhaps it should be translated "assumes a domineering position over the man."

Secondly, she is to be "in silence." She is to be "quiet." That is to say, she is not to teach or preach. Rather, she is to listen. That does not make her a cipher, as some think. We are simply talking about the role that she plays in the structure of the church. After all, it is Christ's church, and He has every right as its King and Head to structure it as He pleases. It just so happens that He decided to do things His way, for His purposes. Who are the "neo-evangelicals" to tell Him otherwise?

What cannot be tolerated is for women to rule over *men.* In Christ's order of things, that is out of order. Nothing allows a woman to bear authority over a man, such as granting her eldership. Elders, as we have seen, are to be "obeyed" (Hebrews 13:17); they "manage" (literally "preside over") Christ's church (1 Thessalonians 5:12, 13), and they "authoritatively instruct" (Titus 2:15) others. It is these things that the "evangelical" feminists are after. They *want* authority over men (over God?)!

This grabbing for power has all but succeeded in the "mainline" liberal churches. This is because, at its core, liberal theology is an attack upon divine authority. It fits their agenda. By seeking to undermine the Bible, they think that they may do away with its authority over them. Feminism seeking church authority blends easily with the spirit of the times and, in general, is but the latest manifestation of the liberals' rejection of the Bible.

The two functions of the elder are to teach and to rule. If a person rejects the authority of Christ in the Scriptures—which Christ said "cannot be broken"—it is a simple matter to reject Paul's words to Timothy by brushing them off with "that's just an old bachelor speaking!" or words to that effect. But for those who claim to accept the Bible as their Standard of faith and practice, to reject apostolic authority is to reject God's Word, and thereby to give a lie to their stated belief in inerrant inspiration. They can't have it both ways. So they make up weak, flawed reasons for finding that the passage teaches something other than what it teaches. Actually, every one of those that is offered fails because of the reasons that Paul gives for his statements in verses 13 and 14. Those reasons – the creation order and the fall in which Eve was deceived – make no sense unless Paul was teaching that, because of these two reasons, women are forbidden authoritative leadership that involves teaching and ruling.

"Okay, I can see that what you have said is true enough concerning elders, but I understand that you think women may become deacons. Isn't that a concession on your part that makes you every bit as guilty of bucking biblical authority as the liberals and the avant-garde evangelicals?"

No, it is not. One is a matter of the rejection of scriptural authority, and the other is a matter of the rejection of faulty exegesis.

"What do you mean by that?"

There are those of us who believe that it is the Bible that opens the office of deacon to women, whereas that same Bible closes the office of elder to them. That is a great difference.

"That clinches it! You *do* believe in women in office!"

I am glad that you brought up the widely used phrase, "women in office," as you did, because it is one that has confused many. Those who forbid women a place in the diaconate often wave it about triumphantly as a clear indication that women may not be deacons.

"Well, why shouldn't they? If women are allowed to hold a church office, that undercuts all that Paul wrote in 1 Timothy 2 about authority, doesn't it?"

No, it doesn't. To argue that way is to assume that those in office— *all* offices—have authority over men. But that just isn't so. The phrase "women in office" originated among people from the Christian Reformed Church where, in the consistory, both elders and deacons meet jointly, the latter in a capacity similar to "junior elders." This situation lends some semblance of truth to the argument that deacons hold an author-itative office—but that is a serious error. And to think of the diaconate as a training ground for elders compounds it! Those who think that way have a very faulty concept of the diaconate.

Office, *per se*, does not carry authority as many seem to think. That is the false premise behind your reasoning. The word "office" simply means "work," and refers to the work to which one is appointed—whatever that may be. When anyone is "ordained" (set apart[3]) to an office, that means that he or she is appointed to a task. The office (work) of an elder involves ruling the church and officially teaching the Scriptures to its members. But the work of the deacon is quite different.

What do deacons do? First, let it be said at the outset: *deacons do not exercise authority.* They are not appointed to a task that requires authority in order to be carried out. They do not rule, and they are not official expositors of the Word.

"Well then, what *do* they do?"

They are to be (as the word literally means) "those who wait on an-other to do his bidding." The work of the deacon is restricted to serving Christ and His church *by serving the elders.*

---

3   Ordination is merely an appointment. There is nothing magical about it. Nothing is conferred but the obligations pertaining to the task. Ordination does not confer authority unless the task itself demands it.

The origin of the diaconate is described in Acts 6:1-7. It was born out of necessity. What was it? That tables had to be served? No. That was but the *occasion* for the formation of the diaconate, and the diaconate filled the need. But the principle behind the formation of this body was much larger: the apostles refused to leave the work to which they were called to do another sort of work. They said, "It isn't right for us to stop preaching God's Word to serve tables" (Acts 6:2). They did not think that it was "beneath" them to take care of the widows, but they recognized that doing so would keep them from the work to which Christ called them. They could not do both. So, having formed the diaconate, they could then say, "We will continue to devote ourselves to prayer and the ministry [literally "deaconing"] of the Word."[4] So the "work" to which they were appointed was to handle a task that, if done by the elders, would have kept them from *their* appointed task (v. 2-4).

Whenever elders find themselves tempted to stray from the work of serving the Word to do some non-authoritative task, they may hand over this latter work to the deacons instead of attending to the pressing need. The diaconate, then, is a catch-all body, the one purpose of which is *to serve the elders* so that they can get on with the tasks to which they were called and ordained.

"Well, what do you know! I never thought of it that way."

Many have not and, as a result, have only confused matters for themselves and for others. You see, all offices are not alike. Some involve work that requires authority to discharge. A person appointed to an office, simply put, is appointed to a particular work. To bring both offices – elder and deacon – together as if they required the same sort of work is to vitiate the very reason for the establishment of the diaconate. And to claim that both are offices requiring *exousia* is an egregious error.

"Okay. I'm tracking with you now. You may be right. But how do women fit into this office of deacon? You said that it was a matter of exegesis and interpretation, didn't you?"

---

4   Here is a play on the word "to deacon." The idea is that because the newly formed deacons were serving (deaconing) tables, they could serve (deacon) the Word. The word is used throughout the passage in the original.

Right! The debate is an exegetical one. It has nothing to do with Political Correctness. It did not originate with the feminists, though, granted, they have used it to further their cause. The issue goes back as far as the Reformation. Calvin and others advocated the position that women may be deacons. The feminists want to use the diaconate as a wedge for moving next into the eldership. And those who hold that the diaconate is an authoritative task similar to that of an elder only give them ammunition that they think fits their guns. In the Christian Reformed Church, where the idea of "women in office" is current, that is precisely what has happened. But, biblically speaking, the diaconate is a totally non-authoritative office. It is an office calling merely for service.

"I can see that, but exegetically, how can you say that women should be eligible for service in the diaconate?"

Many become bogged down discussing 1 Timothy 3:8-13. While a faithful interpretation of the passage leads to the conclusion that women may be deacons, the issue does not stand or fall with what I Timothy 3 says. Also, take a look at Romans 16:1-2, where Paul opens the chapter with these words:

> Now I want to introduce to you Phoebe, our sister, who is a deaconess [literally, "deacon"] from the church of Cenchrea, so that you may receive her in the Lord in a way that is fitting for saints, and help her in any matter in which she may need your assistance, since she, indeed, has been a benefactor of many, including me.

There are a number of things that may be pointed out from an analysis of these two verses. Presumably, Phoebe faithfully carried the letter from Paul to Rome. It might be possible to translate the word *diakonos* as "female servant," but since she is designated "a sister," it is unlikely that Paul would have repeated himself in that way. No, she was a deacon in the church of Cenchrea. She is to be welcomed as a deacon.[5]

Here, we see her about to carry out some task that had been assigned to her by the elders of her church. We have no idea what this was. Paul

---

5   The feminine, *diakonissa*, is used only in ecclesiastical Greek.

knew her well and had benefited from her help in the past. He now explains that she may need the help of the Christians in Rome to carry out the work that she was sent by her church to do. Once more, we see the service of the deacon, here assisting others. Moreover, Phoebe is introduced in a different manner from the other women mentioned in the chapter, placing her in a different category. And, of course, she is mentioned first in the list of those to be commended. Finally, notice that Phoebe doesn't come to the church in Rome, asserting her authority as a deaconess (she had none). She is *"from the church* at Cenchrea." That is to say, she was sent by the authority of the elders there. And to boot, she needs the recommendation of an apostle. There is nothing authoritative about her as a deacon whatsoever! Everything indicates that Phoebe was just what Paul says, "a deacon from the church of Cenchrea" who was on some assignment from the church to which she belonged. There is no reason to believe otherwise, and every reason to believe she bore the title of the office to which she belonged.

In his commentary on this passage, Calvin does not hesitate to call Phoebe an *"assistant* of the Cenchrean church" and says that Paul "commends her on account of her *office."* And he also references 1 Timothy 5:9 as a further indication of the sort of "service" (*diakonia*) in which Phoebe had been involved in her office. Whether we can agree with the way that Calvin reconstructed Phoebe's "office" is unimportant. The crucial point is that, in Reformation times, there was no hesitancy on his part to believe that Phoebe was a deacon and had been called to an office of Christ's church. So you can readily see from the brief discussion of the diaconate that there can be a fine fit between women and the non-authoritative office. Good men, since the outset of the Protestant church, have differed about whether or not women belong in it, but they have differed on exegetical grounds.

Once more, we have seen attempts on the part of women to arrogate authority to themselves. But what is significant is that through their misinterpretation of the office as one involving authority, true Bible-believing Christians, who think that they are opposing liberalism and feminism, actually lend support to those causes. Rather than lump together deacons and elders in order to exclude women from the diaconate, they should more carefully distinguish the elements involved in the work of each. Elders are set apart to the work of teaching and ruling—authoritative tasks. Deacons are ordained to serve the elders by relieving them of any work extraneous to their tasks.

Should a deacon, man or woman, act as if his or her office grants authority to give orders in a high-handed manner, he/she should be rebuked by the elders. The overriding characteristic of a faithful deacon is helpfulness. Understood scripturally, the diaconate is a very helpful office in the church, and women, who already do much diaconal work without an appointment to the office, can be a most useful part of that body. Let's not forbid them to minister to the elders, many of whom are bogged down with all sorts of things they should not have to do.

From 1 Timothy 2, we have clearly seen that authority is not to be given to women; it seems equally true that women may be set aside (ordained) for non-authoritative work. And, of course, such work does not collide with the prohibitions of 1 Timothy 2. Jesus Christ did not set up two authoritative offices that would inevitably conflict with one another. All authority lies in the eldership. Indeed, since there can be no clash of authority in a properly functioning congregation, there ought to be a fruitful working harmony between the two bodies. That is the goal. Does your church approximate it?

YES, it all comes down to this: God is the Authority, the Source of all true authority, and the Determiner of all authority issues. He alone has the right and the ability to set standards for His church; how does anyone else dare do so? Yet that is precisely the problem; all sorts of people within the church have determined that by passing laws, shaming others, setting up lists of dos and don'ts, and the like, they can dictate what is best for the church. They set themselves up as authorities. How dare they muscle their way like that? Yet with little or no compunction, they *do* dare to do so!

Consider this: how many books do you read that attempt to ferret out what *God* has to say in His Word concerning His authority over His church? Perhaps, if you are like many others, this book is the very first that you have ever read that has that goal in mind. The matter is of little interest in the church. And, even here, this book opens up biblical principles and practices relative to authority only to a minimal extent. Much more needs to be said.

Go to the local bookstore. What will you find? If you read anything that directly has to do with authority at all, you will be fortunate. But if you have the eyes to see, what book after book is doing is dealing indirectly with authority issues all the time—without noting the fact. Indeed, many of the authors themselves don't have the slightest idea of that fact. Instead, without any biblical grounds,[1] you will find piles of books that will tell you what to do in the church of Christ and how to do it.

In addition to books, the ideas of men, filched from business practices and propagated in large "spiritual" conferences by "pastoral" CEOs, have spread widely around the church as a whole. Yet most of these concepts are not only inconsistent with biblical teaching, they are antithetical to

---

1   That is to say, without any authority behind what they say but themselves!

it. God's authority is set aside for man's. But if you were to say this, you would be labeled a fundamentalist fanatic. Or if, for some remote reason, someone took your concern seriously and looked into the principles and practices that he is being taught, it is very likely that he could not discern anything wrong with them. He would know so little of the Scriptures that he could not use them to evaluate the material. Many talk about the Bible as a standard, but wouldn't know how to use it as such if you were to spell it out in children's blocks! They are virtually ignorant of wide ranges of truth and have no idea about how to extract it from holy Scripture and apply it to everyday life! Behind all of this is an abysmal lack of concern about knowing God's Word.

After all is said and done, if God *is* the Authority – as you know He is, Christian – then you and others like you must become far more able and eager to discover and put into practice God's authoritative principles, which He has established to guide the mission of His church.

That, for many, means getting far more serious about Bible study. I said *study*, not reading. Reading some daily "devotional" won't do it. Listening to religious broadcasts won't do it. Reading books based on someone's experiences won't do it. It means hours spent every week poring over the pages of Scripture with the best Bible study helps available. It means becoming aware through that study of the many flawed ways in which Christ's work is carried on. It means doing whatever is necessary to correct erroneous ways. Finally, it means putting in place those biblical principles and practices that are authorized by Christ Himself.

After reading this book, how eager are you to do whatever it takes to help your congregation conform to the ways that God has authoritatively ordained? If so, here are some things you might do:

1. Begin to pray about the problems as you come to see them through regular, serious Bible study.
2. Continue to sharpen your understanding of your church's problems through careful Bible study – areas where the church is operating according to unauthorized standards.
3. By continued study, try to determine exactly what God wants done to remedy the situation.

4. Think about non-disruptive ways in which you can mention to the elders of your church what you have learned, and how you think that the problems can be solved. Carping criticism is *not* helpful.

5. Continue to pray and, in a kindly, helpful way, encourage those in charge to take their authority seriously enough to do what God requires of them.

6. *Be patient*; in time, God could use you to bring about the needed change.

7. Above all things, do not become divisive. Don't gather a group together to try to pressure the authorities; don't start complaining all over the church. Rather, talk to God about the matter.

8. All in all, if you follow some such plan in a church that is basically committed to the Scriptures as the inerrant and sufficient Word of God, you may expect good results. If, on the other hand, you are in a congregation that refuses even to acknowledge the Bible as its standard of faith and practice (let alone use it that way), you'd better think about moving to another congregation that is sound in the faith.

Whatever you do, always stand behind and submit to true authority. Enhance it by your life and by your words. Never do anything to denigrate it in the eyes of others. There is all too little authority in the church; when you find some, rejoice, be grateful, and ask God to multiply it! When God's authority in all things is recognized in the church, when He is given His rightful place, He blesses. Does your church need blessing from Him? Could it be that the reason it lacks blessing is because of its lack of true authority from God?

The Use of the Rod and the Staff

A Neglected Aspect of Shepherding

INTRODUCTION

WHEN the Lord ordered Zechariah, "Again, take for yourself the equipment of a foolish shepherd" (Zechariah 11:15), He did not specify what it was that He had in mind. But it seems obvious from the wording of this command that there were shepherds who foolishly took with them wrong implements when they went forth to shepherd sheep. In every occupation there are some who attempt to carry out their work in foolish, and even harmful, ways. Presumably, these pieces of equipment carried by foolish shepherds made it impossible to do the work of shepherding as it should have been done and, consequently, placed the sheep under their care in jeopardy.

There may have been many types of inadequate and, therefore, foolishly acquired items that were substituted for proper implements, but though we have no idea what God had in mind, we clearly do know of some of the *proper* equipment a shepherd ought to carry with him. In Psalm twenty-three, for instance, we read, "Your rod and Your staff comfort me." Since these pieces of shepherdly equipment, in particular, are mentioned in the Scriptures in a positive way, we shall examine carefully what was meant by such *comfort* and how these *implements* brought it about. In addition, we shall inquire somewhat closely about the implements themselves. Moreover, in applying the Scriptures to the contemporary shepherds (pastors, or elders) in our churches, we must also learn what the purposes of such passages may be and how these relate to them today.

All in all, it is an interesting and important study on which we shall embark. Shepherding is a large theme in the Bible, and there is much that could be said about it. But in spite of that, little is made of the shepherd's *equipment*, how he must use it, and what that means for spiritual shepherds in the church today. While in no way minimizing other aspects of his work, it is this part of the shepherd's task upon which we wish to focus. It is a work that is largely neglected not only because too little is made of it, but also because even in those congregations where it is acknowledged as vital.

I wrote *The Use of the Rod and the Staff* principally for pastors and elders, but other members of churches should also understand what the Bible has to say about the matters discussed so that they may know when this shepherdly function is necessary, and see that it is faithfully carried out in their congregations.

As we consider passages that pertain to the equipment of a faithful shepherd and discuss how God expects him to use that equipment, it will be important for those who read to examine the shepherding ministry in their own congregations in the light of biblical teaching. There are all too many places today where, if the shepherding ministry doesn't involve the use of the implements of a foolish shepherd, it surely does lack the presence and use of the wise shepherd's rod and staff.

In order to explicate and apply the subject, from time to time, I shall illustrate scriptural teaching by the use of contemporary examples. It is not these examples in particular to which I wish to call attention—although perhaps the reader will be warned by their use—but it is the principles illustrated that are of prime importance. The purpose of this book is to show the urgency of the matter and thereby to alert every shepherd to a full consideration and implementation of the biblical ministry of using the rod and the staff. As Paul wrote to Archippus, "Be sure that you carry out *to the full* the work of service that you received for the Lord" (Colossians 4:17, emphasis mine).

Jay Adams, 2001

Enoree, SC

CHAPTER 1
THE SHEPHERD AND HIS SHEEP

Before attempting to discuss the use of the shepherd's rod and staff, it will be important to say something of shepherding as it was carried on in Palestine in biblical times. The rich imagery growing out of the task of shepherding that unfolds on the pages of the Bible is the fullest of all;[1] no other imagery is worked out in such detail. Almost every aspect of shepherding is tapped in order to extrapolate upon the various relations of God to His people. It is for this reason that a knowledge of biblical shepherding is important.

Principally, the shepherd is the symbol of *care and concern*. In the opening words of Psalm 23, we see this enthymeme: "The Lord is my Shepherd; I shall not lack." An enthymeme is a syllogism with one of its members missing. The full syllogism would look something like this:

- The Lord is my Shepherd.
- Shepherds meet all of the needs of their sheep.
- Therefore, I shall not lack.

This *caring* aspect of shepherding runs throughout the Bible. It is dominant. For instance, in Zechariah 11:16, the verse following the one quoted in the Introduction, we read that the worthless shepherd "will not visit the perishing, seek the scattered, heal the injured, or feed the healthy." These were some of the normal caring activities of a wise shepherd. But the foolish shepherd mentioned here would not engage in everyday shepherdly concerns. The sum total of this neglect meant that he refused to *care* for his sheep.

The word "visit" in the verse above means *to be concerned about, to give attention to*, not merely to pay a visit to the location where the sheep may be. It may be very readily translated *care for*. In James 1:27, for example, we read that "Clean and undefiled religion before God the Father is to

---

1   There are over 500 references to sheep and flocks in the Scriptures.

visit orphans and widows in their affliction" (ESV). The word "visit" that James used, is related to the term "vision," and also means *to look after*. Surely, paying house calls on widows and orphans is not what he had in mind! Rather, it is about *caring for and looking after* these defenseless persons by protecting them and meeting their needs, that James wrote.

The "worthless shepherd," according to Zechariah 11:17, also "leaves the flock." That just about sums up the most heinous thing that the prophet could say about a shepherd. A good shepherd would never leave helpless sheep to fend for themselves. But here, Zechariah's worthless shepherd not only leaves them to find their own way and exposes them to the mercy of the beasts of prey around them, but—even worse—the shepherd himself "devours the flesh of the fat sheep and tears off their hoofs!"[2] (v. 16). He "shepherds" the sheep only for the advantages *he* may receive from doing so. His concern is not for the sheep, but for himself![3]

So, providing those things that a sheep cannot do for itself is the essence of shepherdly care. It includes leading the flock to food and drink (Psalm 23:2, 3) and in the right paths (v. 3); it means rescuing the lost sheep (even the hundredth); it requires healing those sheep that are wounded; and it involves protecting the flock from wild animals (cf. Jeremiah 50:6, 7). These are prominent among the tasks of good shepherding.

Now, it is against that background that we shall look at the equipment of a good shepherd—in particular, the rod and the staff—and its use. But first, let's ask, "What does caring for the sheep have to do with ministry?"

---

2   That is, he can't get enough to eat otherwise, so he even eats the hoofs! The extent of wickedness of this shepherd is what is pictured.

3   See also Isaiah 5:11ff.

CHAPTER 2

CARING FOR GOD'S FLOCK

S OMEONE asked, "Which is the greater problem in the church—lack of knowledge or apathy?" The answer came back, "I don't know, and I don't care!" That attitude fairly sums up the reasons for many of the difficulties that we shall be dealing with in this book. There is a large share of both ignorance and apathy—culpable ignorance of what the Bible teaches about shepherdly care and indifference on the part of those who know. It will be the task of this volume both to instruct and to exhort. The goal in mind is to arouse concern for shepherdly care—especially in the area of the use of the rod and the staff.

As we have seen, the shepherd imagery extends to feeding, leading, counseling, and guarding the flock. Applied to pastors in today's church, the feeding aspect has to do with *teaching* God's people His will. In Ephesians 4:11, we are told that one of God's gifts to the church is the "shepherd-teacher." There are four offices mentioned in the verse, not five. God gave His church apostles and prophets as well as evangelists (an office that includes the work of present-day missionaries) and pastor-teachers. This last office is hyphenated because in the original, it is clear that the two terms "pastor" (which is another word for "shepherd") and "teacher" refer to the same office. The apostles and prophets filled extraordinary, temporary offices by laying the foundation for the church (Ephesians 2:20),[1] particularly in a revelatory way.[2] The ordinary offices of evangelist and shepherd-teacher remain.

Why would the last office be described in this two-fold manner? Because within the one *office*, there are two *functions*. According to 1

---

1   For more details on this matter see my book *Signs and Wonders in the Last Days.*
2   See also Ephesians 3:5, where we read of information that "has been revealed to His holy apostles and prophets by the Spirit."

Timothy 5:17,[3] all who are called to the office of elder "rule" or "manage" and, in addition, some elders also teach (they are involved in "preaching and teaching"). Thus, all elders are to *function* as rulers in the church; of them, only some *function* also as teachers and preachers. These elders are the ones to whom God entrusts His flock. They are to manage, guide, and teach the sheep. When shepherds fail to carry out those shepherdly functions as they should, the flock suffers.

Sheep are naturally stupid. One theologian who lived with a shepherd in Palestine told me that they are so foolish that they will eat themselves lost. So long as they find grass they will go on eating it, regardless of where this may take them, even if they leave the rest of the flock behind. Sheep need the everyday oversight[4] of a shepherd who lives with and guides them so as to see to it that they don't do such things. Isaiah attested to this "straying" character of sheep when he wrote "All of us *like sheep* have gone *astray*. Each of us has turned to his own way" (Isaiah 53:6, KJV). That is why the sheep often get "lost." Of course, poor shepherding itself also may lead to such a condition: "My people have become lost sheep; their shepherds have led them astray" (Jeremiah 50:6). The tragic fact—that shepherds lead sheep astray[5]—is, as we shall see, one of the reasons why it is necessary to write a book such as this one.

Guiding, also, is a chief task of shepherds. True pastors counsel the individual members of their flocks about how they may find and walk in the "ways of righteousness" for God's sake. And to accomplish this, they train them to do so (2 Timothy 3:16). They not only "teach" all that Christ "commanded," but assist the members of the flock to "observe" those commandments.[6] They help those who lose their way find the

---

3   "The elders who manage well should be considered worthy of double pay, especially those who are laboring at preaching and teaching." The word in the King James translated "honor" (*time*) may also be translated "pay." That "pay" is the correct translation is clear from verse 18 in which the rationale for it is given from the Old Testament.
4   "Bishop" is the other biblical word that is used to designate the office of the shepherding elder (cf. Titus 1:5-7; Acts 20:17, 28, where the words "elder" and "bishop" are used interchangeably).
5   Or, at best, allowing others to do so without adequate biblical response. The apathy of shepherds in this regard is appalling
6   See also Matthew 27:20, 21. For details, see my book *Teaching to Observe*.

way back to God through repentance and biblical guidance. They work with and restore those who are ruining their lives. They spend much time "counseling" out of deep concern for God and His people (cf. Acts 20:31).[7] This is because they are *devoted* to their flocks.

But it is also the task of the shepherd to *protect* his flock. Paul spoke of "fierce wolves" that would enter the church after his departure, and others who would arise "from among" themselves, "not sparing the flock," in order "to drag away disciples to follow them."[8] He urged *alertness* because of this fact. To be alert for false teaching, division, and schismatic tendencies is also a vital responsibility that impinges upon elders. How vital, we are about to see. Yet many "shepherds," though not apathetic, are ignorant and fearful of the important task of defending helpless sheep from attack.

But the question now arises, "If these are shepherdly tasks, how do these tasks relate to the equipment that is called by David—who knew all about shepherding a flock of sheep—the "rod and the staff?"

---

7   The apostle Paul said, "Therefore, be alert, remembering that for three years, night and day, I didn't stop counseling each one of you with tears."
8   Paul's words echo those of his Lord Who spoke of "wolves in sheep's clothing" (Matthew 7:15). We might add that there are also wolves in shepherd's clothing!

CHAPTER 3
NOW, ABOUT THAT EQUIPMENT

W E saw from Zechariah 11:15 that God called the prophet, who previously had faithfully shepherded his people, now to act symbolically like a shepherd who attempted to carry out his work in a "foolish" manner. He was to take up the wrong implements. These were instruments that a foolish shepherd might carry with him when going out with his sheep. What specific instruments these were is not of significance to us, or God would have had his prophet clearly state their exact nature. What is important, however, is the *fact of foolishness* in using equipment that, obviously, wouldn't get the job done and would, therefore, endanger the sheep.

There are those who, in attempting to shepherd God's flock in His churches today, also foolishly use the wrong equipment.[1] That this is so is a matter that should concern us. Any pastor who fails to use the proper implements of a shepherd will serve his flock poorly, will place them in jeopardy and, as the result, will exhibit utter foolishness. Pastor, since you are commanded to "shepherd God's flock among you, exercising shepherdly care over it" (1 Peter 5:2), you need to take heed to all that the Bible has to say about proper shepherdly tools—those that are designed to equip a shepherd to meet the exigencies of the work to which God has called him. And the shepherd must not only possess those tools, but he must also know when to use them and how to do so.

Those who ignore what God says about these matters in the Scriptures are truly "foolish." And, to boot, they are unfaithful to God, His people, and their calling as shepherds. Pastor, don't be like Zechariah's foolish shepherd! In order that "when the chief Shepherd appears, you [may] receive the glorious crown that will never fade" (1 Peter 5:4), we shall ex-

---

1   There are various reasons for this: fear, apathy, ignorance, false teaching, or a wrong emphasis on tolerance.

amine what the Scriptures tell you about biblical shepherding equipment and its use. Take to heart what you learn, and apply it in your ministry.

That a shepherd must be well equipped for difficult tasks was, as we shall see, an important matter. The work to which he was called was not merely an intellectual matter; shepherding is not academic.[2] The biblical shepherd had to do dangerous, physical work as well as lead the flock. The spiritual shepherd of the flock likewise must undertake tasks that require far more than academic excellence. He must know how to deal with his people in all their sinful ways. And he must know how to deal with those who would lead them astray.[3]

Like others who depend upon equipment specifically designed to help them carry out their trade, the biblical shepherd's tasks could not be done as they should be without the proper implements peculiar to it. The salesman needs his automobile, the clerk needs her computer, the technician needs his machinery; so, too, the shepherd must have the right equipment. He must have his rod and staff!

It is interesting to examine the Hebrew word that is translated "equipment" or "implements" (as the word *keli* is variously rendered in most versions). The term may refer simply to tools in general, as the two above translations indicate. But, quite frequently, it also refers to armor or weapons. Since, as we shall see, the pieces of equipment that are mentioned in Psalm 23—the rod and the staff (not to mention the shepherd's sling)—are both items that have to do with protection, it may well be that what the prophet Zechariah has in mind is that the foolish shepherd went out unprepared to defend the sheep from harm.

---

2   Too many pastors are trained academically, but lack the practical training of the sort that will be so much a part of their ministry. They, therefore, muddle through without adequate knowledge or skills to truly care for sheep. Not only should seminary training be radically changed, but, until that happens, men who were poorly taught must find ways to make up for this lack. There are now places across the country where training to supplement seminary is being made available. As the seminaries continually fail to train men for shepherding work, such centers and programs are growing in number.

3   For instance, Paul wrote in Titus 1:9–13 that the shepherdly overseer must "be able both to encourage by healthy teaching, and convict of their error those who object." He went on to say, "For this reason, rebuke them sharply, that their faith may remain healthy."

Be that as it may, throughout the prophets—and in the book of Zechariah itself—we see God condemning those shepherds who, rather than defending their sheep from attack by wolves, allow the flock to be scattered and devoured: "the people wander like sheep. They are afflicted, because there is no shepherd. My anger is kindled against the shepherds" (Zechariah 10:2, 3). Here, Zechariah mentions shepherds who abandoned the defenseless sheep, leaving them as prey for wild animals. Perhaps they abandoned the sheep because they would not stand up against the onslaught of the wolf pack. They feared for their *own* lives. And that fear, in turn, might stem from the failure to bring with them the weapons by which they might drive the wolves away. Perhaps a foolish shepherd would reason, "Why carry cumbersome weapons if one has no intention of doing battle?"

In any case, so-called "shepherds" leaving sheep defenseless, as described here in Zechariah, sadly, is a prominent theme in Scripture.[4] Our Lord Jesus Himself spoke of shepherdly attendants like these: "A hired man … leaves the sheep and runs when he sees the wolf coming, and the wolf grabs them and scatters them" (John 10:12). He does so because, as Jesus further explained, "he really doesn't care about the sheep" (v. 13). There are "shepherds" like that in the church today. About all such, God has this to say: "Woe to my worthless shepherd who leaves the flock!" (Zechariah 11:17).[5] The same warning holds true today. Pastor, elder, I beg you to take that warning to heart! They are the instruments of a foolish shepherd!

So, it is altogether possible—but not essential to the message of this volume—that the equipment that the foolish shepherd took along with him was something other than that with which he might defend his flock. Instead of weapons, he might readily have carried equipment that would lend comfort to himself rather than to his sheep. Weapons that promote compromise with heresy, error, and wickedness will bring no comfort to God's sheep.

---

4   Particularly in Zechariah and the other prophets.
5   Indeed, the entire eleventh chapter is an indictment of foolish, worthless shepherds.

Notice that in Psalm 23, we are told that the Shepherd's rod and staff "comfort" the sheep. Here, the sheep and the people who are pictured under the image of sheep blend together. The sheep are thought of as people, reasoning that they are safe because of the implements (weapons) that the Shepherd carries. They find "comfort" in the fact that He possesses them, so that if needed, they are at hand. They are further comforted by the fact that their Shepherd knows how to use them. And lastly, they take comfort in the fact that He is ready and willing to do so! It is the presence or the lack of these things that distinguishes a hired man from a good shepherd. It is these things (or their lack) that preserve the flock and bring honor (or the opposite) to a shepherd. And, as we shall go on to see, it is these same things today (or the lack thereof) that often make the difference between a good and a foolish shepherd of Christ's church.

Since this is true, let us proceed to examine these two implements that are so clearly mentioned as those that the Lord bears as our Shepherd.

CHAPTER 4

THE COMFORTING ROD AND STAFF

In Psalm 23, David speaks of the "comfort" that the shepherd's rod and staff brought his sheep (v. 4). The comfort that he has in view is the ease of mind that comes from a sense of safety. He speaks of "fearing no evil" because of the shepherd's presence (v. 4). How important that comfort is to helpless, defenseless sheep! There is no way that sheep can negotiate the rugged, dangerous terrain in the mountains of Palestine or feed peacefully in the fields of tender green grass without a sense of security. There is too much to fear of their surroundings, especially when roaming alone.

The psalmist, in particular, mentions the "valley of the shadow of death" (v. 4). Mistakenly, many refer this expression to going through the experience of death. But rather than that, it speaks of safety from the threat of death in dangerous situations. As the shepherd and his sheep climbed down into the valleys that separated one mountain from another, they passed many shadowy crevices in which death in the form of wild animals lurked. Alone, without the shepherd to care for them, sheep are utterly helpless. But the sheep in this Psalm gained comfort from the ways in which the good Shepherd used His rod and staff in the past to protect them from danger and death. They knew that when He was present, carrying these instruments, they were safe. No flock of God's sheep should ever have to fear spiritual danger; they will not when a shepherd faithfully wields the rod and the staff.

God's sheep—His people—often act like the animals David shepherded. They too, find it hard to travel through a wearisome, difficult world beset by dangers. This world of sin, with its many pitfalls, is not an easy place in which to live. There is difficulty on every hand. That, of course, is not the way God made it. Indeed, when He created man, God placed him in Paradise, a location called The Garden of Eden (which means, literally, "The park of pleasures"). It was man's rebellion that brought about the difficulties that he now encounters. Because of man's sin, God cursed the world, and it became anything but a place of pleasure. Moreover, it is filled with people who have yielded themselves to the service of the evil one, who in turn hates Christians with a passion and does all that he can to stir up his followers against them (John 8:42ff.).

And—in addition—God's human, partly sanctified sheep are themselves often foolish and obstinate, thereby bringing unnecessary hardships upon themselves. Because of these problems, God has provided earthly shepherds for the members of His church to guide and protect them from the evils that surround them, and from the many foolish and stubborn ways that remain in them. Shepherding is not easy, but those whom God chose as undershepherds must, nevertheless, undertake their *"labor* in the Lord" (1 Thessalonians 5:12). To labor "in" (or "for") Him means that He will provide all that is necessary to do so; one does not have to labor in his own wisdom or strength.

It is because of these difficult problems that will occur that the elders of the church are exhorted to protect the flock from those who would scatter and harm them and are instructed how to do so. Listen again to Paul's words in Acts 20:28 and following, to the elders of the church of Ephesus:

> *Pay attention to yourselves and to all of the flock among which the Holy Spirit has set you to be overseers to shepherd God's church that He acquired with His own blood. I know that after my departure fierce wolves will enter in among you, not sparing the flock, and from among yourselves men will arise speaking distorted things to drag away disciples to follow them. Therefore, be alert ...*

Clearly, this double attack upon the church, from within and from without, has continued over the entire course of church history. Our day is no exception. Because elders failed in the task of protecting the flock from heresy and schism, it was not long until every sort of error imaginable found its way into the church. And the sheep were harassed. The problems began even while the apostles were alive. Letter after letter of the New Testament was sent to individuals and churches to straighten out difficulties of doctrine and life that should have been handled locally by the church elders. But, obviously, these elders failed over and over again as protecting shepherds of their flocks.

In the post-apostolic age, matters quickly grew worse. Heretical teachings such as baptismal regeneration, salvation by works and ceremonies, the worship of saints, the rule of bishops over elders, false prophecy and revelation and, ultimately, the primacy of one bishop [the pope] led to a situation that, by the time of the Reformation, was so serious it was difficult to find the biblical, apostolic faith anywhere in the church. Again, this was the result of elders who did not heed Paul's words and faithfully discharge their duty to protect the flock. If we should learn anything from church history, it is how frequently the elders of the church fail as protecting shepherds. And we should learn how important it is for them to do so!

In our time, once again the evangelical church has grown lax. There is an emphasis upon tolerance that tends to exclude shepherdly protection. In the eyes of many sheep today the "good guy" is the one who makes no protest against unbiblical teachings and practices; the "bad guy" is the one who will not "take part in the unfruitful works of darkness" but instead "goes so far as to expose them" (Ephesians 5:11). The "good guy" is the one who endeavors to go along as far as possible with the world; the "bad guy" is the one who avoids eclecticism at all costs. It is, perhaps, this tolerance of and mixture with worldly principles and practices, and such tolerance of error and heresy that has most seriously affected the Bible-believing churches of our time. All too few elders (including both ruling and teaching elders) are aware of the insidious inroads of worldly thought and practices within the church. If something is not done to correct this situation, however, it is clear that truth once more will be seriously compromised, and if it continues for long unabated, truth may once more all but vanish from the church.

This sense of tolerance and camaraderie with heretical and false teachers may have nearly reached its peak. Now, for instance, even so-called fundamentalists have been hobnobbing with faith healers, self-styled "prophets" and Word of Faith (name it and claim it) teachers. For instance, I was astounded, I confess (though I guess I shouldn't have been), when I read that Jerry Falwell endorsed the ministry of Benny Hinn. Reportedly, he said,

> Pastor Benny and I are friends ... He came [to Lynchburg] and we had a wonderful day together. He met the 6,000 students of Liberty University as we walked from building to building. Most of them knew him. Many of them are your partners [Benny] ... We spent a lot of time in conversation about what God is doing ... I am a Baptist ... When I look at your crowd in those coliseums, all I see are the 18-year-old high school seniors. Now I know the rest are important, but I want all of them at Liberty University to train them to be champions for Christ.[1]

Hinn is notorious for his false prophecies and revelations, his heretical teaching, and his unsubstantiated claims to healings. It was he who, for instance, taught that there are nine members of the "Trinity" (each of the three Members Himself being threefold!). Yet here is Falwell buddying up to him! From Falwell's comment about wanting Hinn's youth for his university, it seems that his main interest in doing so was to try to get more students. If that was the motive, as the quotation seems to indicate, what a shameful compromise it was! Be that as it may, how could he favorably expose his 6,000 students to Hinn as he did? How could he call them "partners" with Hinn? The difference of which he *should* speak is not between Falwell as a Baptist and Hinn—whose present affiliation seems uncertain[2]—but between one who believes the Scriptures and one who teaches heresy. *Partners* with such a person?

Moreover, Falwell calls Hinn a "friend." How he can call him a friend is unfathomable. What sort of friend is Hinn of the true God? God does not befriend those who "have other Gods before Him" (literally, in His face!). And if *they* are not friends, how can Falwell remain a friend of both? Moreover, if Hinn is a false prophet, as is clearly pointed out in *The Confusing World of Benny Hinn*, either Falwell is a compromiser who has put his students at risk by palling around with and endorsing Hinn, or

---

1   Richard Fisher and Kurt Goedelman, *The Confusing World of Benny Hinn.* Morris Publishing, Kearney (2001), p. 1x, x.
2   He was in and out of affiliation with the Assemblies of God.

he is ignorant of Hinn's teachings and practices. Either way, as a shepherd in the church, Falwell has failed to protect the flock!

Hinn is but one example of a sad defection from truth that not only is largely going unexposed, but is being pandered to by evangelicals! And Falwell is not the only one who is not merely tolerant of, but also endorses, people like Hinn. One cannot help but think that the apostle Paul and Benny Hinn would hardly have ended up *friends* after spending "a lot of time" in conversation about God!

Now, because I have mentioned Falwell, some will label me one of the "bad guys." Ask yourself, "Who really is the one at fault?" for the failure to withstand error in the church and the encouragement to compromise with it. Who fails to *expose error and falsehood* for what it is, but rather *exposes the sheep* (and the *lambs*) of the flock to it? You judge!

The problem is that in order to be "good guys," many elders, who doubtless know better, have laid aside their rods and staffs. Instead, they have traded them for the equipment of a foolish shepherd! How important it is for them to rethink what they are doing, once more pick up the proper instruments of defense that they have abandoned, and use them to protect the sheep under their care! If they do not, as we have just seen in the case of Falwell and Hinn, we will not even know where to send our children to school!

But we still have not taken a hard enough look at the rod and the staff, which provide such comfort for the sheep. That comfort is important for the well-being of God's sheep. This we shall now begin to investigate more fully.

Chapter 5

The Shepherd's Staff

O N page 94 of John Davis' informative book, *The Perfect Shepherd*, there is a photograph of a shepherd carrying his "crook."[1] This instrument is a long staff (or pole) with a curve, or hook, at the end.[2] While the Hebrew word for "staff" that occurs in Psalm 23:4 (*misenet*) was used to describe a number of items of the sort, doubtless here, in reference to a shepherd, it refers to the crook which Gower describes as follows:

> The shepherd was equipped with a staff, but it was not a weapon, although it was used on ... occasions [as such]. The staff was about six feet (two metres) long and sometimes had a crook at the end of it. It was normally used to help the shepherd get around easily in hilly or rough country. It was often used *to help control the sheep* (emphasis mine).[3]

John Davis adds,

> I was interested to note that Mohammed Yaseen used his staff to check the crevices in caves in order to chase out snakes or scorpions that might endanger himself or his flock.

Miller and Miller write: "Here they [the sheep] felt the touch of his [the shepherd's] helpful hooked staff, lifting them over perilous stones."[4] Clearly, the staff was one of the shepherd's principal means of protecting and controlling sheep.

But note, especially, the staff was usually used to protect sheep against their *own* foibles and their inability to handle dangerous situations. It

---

1   John J. Davis *The Perfect Shepherd*. Baker Book House, Grand Rapids (1979). Davis lived among Palestinian shepherds for a time and is able to illustrate many of their ways from personal experience.
2   See also the drawing in Ralph Glover's *The New Manners and Customs of Bible Times*. Moody Press, Chicago (1986), p. 137.
3   *Ibid.,* p. 138.
4   Madeline Miller and J. Lane Miller, *The Encyclopedia of Bible Life*. Harper and Brothers, Publisher, New York (1944), p. 34.

was not normally used as a weapon (though it might be employed as the quarter-staff was in later times in Europe). In a sense, then, it corresponds not only to the way a shepherding elder meets personal sins and inadequacies of individual sheep, but perhaps also to Paul's warning about those who would arise from among the flock itself to lead them astray. On these occasions, it became a defensive instrument used to guard the sheep against harm brought on by themselves or by other straying sheep.

There are many ways in which sheep must be guarded against themselves and against other members of the flock. Sheep have a self-centered orientation. As mentioned earlier, sometimes they will eat themselves lost. Forgetting everything else, they will pursue the grass lying before them, eating their way far from the flock. When they have finally filled themselves to satisfaction, they will suddenly become aware that they have left the flock. At this point, they will become frantic, not knowing which way to go to find the shepherd and the rest of the flock. The shepherd must rescue them.

That picture of sheep who have gone astray and turned to their own way (as Isaiah put it) describes us in our self-centered sin. How often we leave the shepherds whom God has placed over us, will not listen to the preaching of the Word, and instead, "do our own thing." When that occurs, we must be protected from ourselves. The ministry of the Word in counseling has been placed in the charge of the elders for this very purpose. Paul wrote:

> *Now we ask you brothers, to recognize those who labor among you, and manage you in the Lord, and counsel you. Think quite highly of them in love because of their work. Be at peace among yourselves (1 Thessalonians 5:12, 13).*

Clearly, there are many straying sheep who, on the one hand, fail to obey this admonition, while, on the other hand, there are too many elders who fail to take their shepherdly managing "work" seriously. The former do not "think highly" of elders, will not submit to and obey them (see Hebrews 13:17) as they seek to "manage" the flock, and fail to heed their counsel. The latter do not warn the flock of dangerous trends in the church, will not go after straying sheep, and will not counsel them when they are perplexed about problems. They have laid aside their staffs. This deplorable situation concerning elders and flocks is what is found in many (should I say "most"?) congregations today! It *must* be remedied. Until it is, and biblical shepherding is reestablished in congregations, the church will become riddled with error and falsehood, and grow farther and farther away from its Lord.

Truth ought to be uppermost in the church. It is on truth that the sheep feed in order to grow. Jesus prayed for His sheep, "Sanctify them by Your truth; Your Word is truth" (John 17:17). Notice two things: truth is essential for sanctification (growing from sin unto righteousness) and that truth is found in the Scriptures. Because there are so many other sources of information abroad today hankering for a hearing, the Christian must *beware* of what he is being taught. And his elders must *be aware* of insidious influences that are being brought to bear upon him so as to warn or rescue him from those dangers into which he may fall.

The problem is, as Paul said, that there will arise from *within* the church many who would lead sheep astray. Every day on television and over the radio, false teaching of every sort, proclaiming to be Christian and biblical, may be heard. Elders of truly Bible-believing churches must become aware of the false teaching that is being propagated at any given time, and must instruct their members as to its unbiblical nature. They should be aware of any members of the congregation who have become so enamored of such error that they have begun to spread it among other members of the flock. They should preach and teach the truth so clearly that error stands out in stark contrast to it. Often, they must name names of false teachers as the apostle Paul frequently did in his letters. Otherwise, the sheep may not know whose teaching they should avoid. Elders may not be neutral about such matters; they must use the crook to snatch one sheep by the leg in order to keep him from falling over a precipice, another from following "a wolf in sheep's clothing." They must keep him out of caves where the devil's snakes and scorpions lie in wait, or clear the cave before allowing him to enter it. When these dangerous creatures have secretly crawled into their midst, they must use their staff to chase them away.

As one examines the situation in today's church, it becomes immediately apparent that there is all too little concern about the protective aspects of shepherding. And where concern does exist, there are all too few who have the courage to stand between the one promoting error and the sheep. They fear the rebuke of those who will accuse them of being heresy-hunters, intolerant, and the like. But a *true* shepherd is always intolerant to the nth degree of the wolf or anything else that may harm his flock!

In short, many sheep today are allowed to go their own way—even when straying into places where they endanger their own spiritual lives and the lives of other sheep around them. Apart from solid teaching from the Scriptures and an alert, concerned eldership, members (and, eventually, whole congregations) will wander into paths of unrighteousness. God knew that it is disastrous for sheep to be left alone. They are defenseless; either they destroy themselves or allow others to destroy them. That is why He placed elder-shepherds, armed with their staffs, in the church.

CHAPTER 6
THE SHEPHERD'S ROD

L IKE the staff, the rod is a piece of defensive equipment. In protecting the flock, shepherds do not instigate a battle with wolves or attack offensively; they withstand the attack of the wolf, the bear, and the lion so that the wild beast cannot get in among the flock. The rod is the principal weapon of defense in this regard. A stout oak stick, that is larger at the business end from which nails protrude, is the sort of instrument about which we are speaking. It hung by the shepherd's side on a thong suspended from his belt. With it, he could do great damage to any marauding beast, as David did, even killing it:

> And David said to Saul, "Your servant was tending his father's sheep.
> When a lion or a bear came and took a lamb from the flock, I went out
> after him and struck him, and rescued it from his mouth; and when he
> rose up against me, I seized him by his beard and struck him and killed
> him.[1] Your servant has killed both the lion and the bear" (1 Samuel
> 17:34–36, NASB).

Clearly, this account is one from which today's elder-shepherd should learn. He, too, is called to fight bears and lions!

The account does not specify how David killed the bear and the lion, but there is no reason to think that he did so with his bare hands. Since it is David himself who speaks of the rod and the staff, there is every reason to think that he used his rod to strike and fell these wild animals. The fact that he took the animal by his beard further substantiates the fact that he was too close to have used the sling (the shepherd's other weapon mentioned in the Bible), leaving the rod as the weapon of choice. In any case, from Psalm 23, it is clear that David thought highly of the

---

1   Presumably with his rod (emphasis mine).

rod as a powerful weapon with which to bludgeon any attacking animal.

Ought shepherds beat the life out of wolves in sheep's clothing? Yes. Not physically, of course. The weapons of our warfare are not carnal. But by every biblically legitimate means they ought to do battle with, and subdue, and drive them far from the sheep. David does not speak in vain of God as a Shepherd Who uses a rod against those who attack His people. And all of the shepherdly imagery that is applied to men by the prophets makes it just as clear that it is their duty to protect the sheep by dealing summarily with wolves.

We have seen in earlier chapters that shepherds who fail to do so are called "worthless," because they leave the flock when it is attacked. And the testimony of Jesus in John 10 to the nefarious nature of such flight is also recorded. The expectation everywhere is that a faithful shepherd will stand by his flock in times of danger to protect them from any and all onslaughts, even at the cost of his life.[2] Do Christian shepherds do this today? Or do most of them fall into the condemnation of being "foolish shepherds" and the "hired men?"

Before seeking an answer to this question, let us consider how one does battle with a wolf, lion, or bear in sheep's clothing. Certainly, nothing physical is in view, as we said. Jesus told us that His kingdom is not of this world and indicated that, since it is not, His servants would not fight physically to preserve and propagate it. Well, then, what is the equivalent of the rod today? Certainly, the pulpit must be one modern manifestation of the use of the rod. False beliefs that would injure the flock must be exposed and, in preaching, beaten down with Scripture. The use of the computer to write and publish is another means of using the rod. When error is publicly set forth in the name of Jesus Christ, it is incumbent upon every shepherd who has the opportunity and ability to do so to expose this error as such, and name the names of those who propagate it. Paul did this so that the flock would be able to distinguish between true shepherds and false ones. Counseling elders should point out error and refute false teaching. It is the use of Christ's Word—the

---

2   Few today would lose their lives by protecting sheep from wolves. But they may lose their friends and their reputations as "good guys" among those who disdain any hostility toward those who attack God's sheep!

rod of His mouth (Isaiah 11:4)—that he uses.

But does it happen today? Well, yes, in some venues. But all too infrequently. Take the following cases, for instance. Process Theology (or, as it is currently called, Open Theology) has invaded formerly evangelical schools. This theological belief, that God takes risks because He supposedly learns along with man what will take place in the future, is nothing short of heresy. Such men as Clark Pinnock, Richard Rice, John Sanders, and others espouse and propagate this view. How often has there been a reference to this heretical form of theism from the pulpit? Have you heard about it? Yet books, like *The Openness of God: A Biblical Challenge to the Traditional Understanding of God,* which is published by Intervarsity Press, are recommended to young people in colleges and universities and sold in Christian bookstores.[3] The enemy of true theism has invaded the church and laid down the "challenge." Will shepherds take it up?

That they should use the rod of Scripture to demolish these heretical views is certain. The Bible teaches no such thing as the "Openness" that these heretics set forth. Yet, note that they claim to have a biblical basis for their theology. That is what makes their view dangerous. But how many heretics have not made the same claim? By ignoring answers that for centuries have been given to questions pertaining to anthropomorphic language, Open Theology advocates sweep uninformed believers off their feet. Pastors and teachers ought to make their congregations aware of the existence of this movement and how the church has handled the seeming problems that they have raised.

Surely, when preaching about the sovereignty or the omniscience of God, a faithful minister will refute the feeble notion of Richard Rice who wrote, "In order to affirm creaturely freedom, the open view of God maintains that certain aspects of the future are yet indefinite ... And this means that God's knowledge of the future cannot be exhaustive."[4] The god set forth in this statement is not the God of the Bible. Shall we tolerate teaching of this nature as "merely another viewpoint?" or should

---

3   Many "Christian" bookstores are mine fields. One must be careful of every step!
4   Richard Rice, *God's Foreknowledge and Man's Free Will.* Bethany House Publishers, Minneapolis (1985), p. 53. Surely, true theists ought to avoid buying books from the presses that propagate such teaching.

we regard it as dangerous to the welfare of our congregations? What is Intervarsity doing in releasing such materials? Should elders make their congregations aware of the fact that books coming from a previously sound source can no longer be trusted to be biblical? Surely, the shepherds ought to awaken and take notice! And—in every way possible—use the rod to drive off such teaching from the flock!

These examples might be multiplied many times over. Indeed, before finishing the discussion in this book, I shall mention some others. But for now, think hard, Elder; are you doing all you can to protect the flock that God has placed in your charge?

N OT every place where the Lord speaks of dealing with false doctrine is cast in the mold of shepherding. Yet, apart from the imagery, the same principles are always set forth. Let us consider a few such passages. For instance, in 1 Timothy 4:1, 2, and 6, Paul writes:

> *Now here are the words that the Spirit speaks plainly: that in times later on some will turn away from the faith by paying attention to deceiving spirits and teachings of demons, through the hypocrisy of liars whose consciences have become desensitized as if they were seared by a hot iron ... If you advise the brothers about these things you will be a good servant of Christ Jesus....*

Now, notice more closely. What does Paul recommend? Avoiding the problem? No. Calling the teaching of demons "alternate views" to be considered? Certainly not. Treating those who turn away as hopeless? Indeed not. Avoiding calling deception what it is—deception? Read the passage. Does he refer to those who lie to members of the flock in order to cause them to turn away as "erring brothers"? Not on your life! Paul calls them deceiving spirits, liars, and hypocrites without consciences. He minces no words.

But what does he *do* about the problem? And what is it he tells Timothy to do? He exposes the problem and the troublemakers, describing them for exactly what they are. He commands Timothy to "advise the brothers about these things." When he does so, Timothy is to use the same plain speaking that the Spirit and Paul used to describe these false teachers. Though others may call him harsh, when an elder does these things, Jesus will consider him a "good servant."

Clearly, if we were to place the truths taught in this passage into a shepherding context, we would be told that a good shepherd *advises* sheep about false teachers who will turn from Christianity and teach demonic beliefs. But that is precisely where people hesitate today. They consider such "advice" heresy hunting! But to obey Paul's command would mean that some of those who have set forth these teachings would not only be exposed for their false teachings, but also that they would be shown to be hypocrites and liars who have little or no pangs of conscience about what they are doing to God's sheep. Doubtless, this advice would also contain powerful scriptural arguments used as a rod to demolish the errors propagated and to establish the sheep in the truth. The rod would be employed so effectively by a faithful elder that he would "stop their mouths," as Paul told Titus to do (Titus 1:11).

Obviously, this way of thinking is foreign to many today. They almost bristle at the thought of speaking about false teachers, let alone using such language. But when the Spirit speaks plainly, and when Paul echoes Him, we had better rethink our contemporary Casper Milquetoast approach to the problem.[1] Who has the right to define what a "good servant of Christ Jesus" is? Is it those who criticize faithful shepherds as heresy hunters, or is it Christ, the Chief Shepherd, addressing us through His inspired apostles?

Paul was concerned about Timothy's reticence. He continually encouraged him to be forthright. In 2 Timothy 1:6 and 7, for instance, he wrote:

> For this reason I remind you to rekindle into a flame God's gift that is in you through the laying on of my hands; I say this because God didn't give a spirit of cowardice, but of power and of love and of self-restraint.

There is too much cowardice in the church disguised as kindness, tolerance, sophistication, and objectivity. The excuses cover up a basic fear of stating hard truths and confronting spiritual wolves. But the elder of Christ need not fear the opposition. God has given all of His shepherds those things that are necessary to fulfill every aspect of the ministry to which He called them—including the use of the rod and the staff (2

---

1   Consider also Paul's words in 1 Timothy 6:3–5.

Timothy 3:17). In the Scriptures, as these passages make clear, there are directions for dealing with error and those who teach it. We are to follow them.

Listen also to these words in Romans 16:17-18:

> *Now I urge you, brothers, to watch out for those who, by disregarding the teaching that you have learned, cause divisions and give occasions for stumbling. Keep away from them. Such people don't serve the Lord Christ as His slaves, but are slaves of their own appetites and by fine talk and flattery they deceive the hearts of the unsuspecting.*

Again, using shepherding terminology, the passage encourages shepherd-elders to lead flocks away from dangerous wild animals that might scatter and devour them. It does not speak kindly of these false teachers who "deceive the hearts of the unsuspecting" (helpless, dumb sheep). Rather, these teachers are described as self-oriented. They care nothing for the flock; they are interested only in satisfying their own appetites. Again, *deception* is a problem that will be encountered over and over again.

In setting forth these things, it is not that we wish to be unkind to others. Nor do we rejoice in detecting heresy. If possible, we would always hope to win those who "oppose" the truth (2 Timothy 2:25). It is not pleasant to have to deal with such people, but we must do so if we would be faithful shepherds. Neither Paul nor anyone else wants to vilify those who cause the flock to "stumble." But, because true shepherds must put the flock first, and view heretics and schismatics as nothing less than wolves who seek to devour the sheep in Christ's "little flock," they must expose and oppose them for what they are. That note of deep concern for the sheep is what is missing in so many churches today. The feeble note struck instead is, "Let us all learn to live in peace with one another even though we differ;" or "I don't say you're wrong; it's just that we differ."

How one addresses the problem of false teaching is a matter of his perspective. If he has been so influenced by contemporary pluralism that he cannot tell a wolf from a shepherd, he will call for peace between the two. If his orientation is biblical, he will see nothing but stark contrast and enmity between them. True shepherds will never allow the sheep to be attacked without attempting to protect them. They will, therefore, always carry the rod—and use it!

In addition to those passages quoted above, listen to this one in which Paul—after listing a whole host of their sins—says that people will have "a form of godliness, but [reject] its power" (2 Timothy 3:5). If any one phrase describes the present condition of much so-called Christianity that is it! In that same verse, he commands "turn away from such people." There is no question about it; rather than hobnob or fellowship with them, we must avoid them. Cooperative efforts must not be countenanced. He then writes:

> *From among people like these are those who worm their way into houses and capture weak women who are loaded with sins and led by all sorts of desires, who are always learning and never able to come to a knowledge of the truth (2 Timothy 3:6, 7).*

Without a doubt, those words describe a number of people in our day. They run from conference to conference, become enamored with this speaker and that, read books containing every sort of wild idea, and listen avidly to radio and TV preachers who advocate many false views. As a result, they are confused and never settle down to the truth. As the text indicates, they are desire-driven, so that whatever sounds warm and pleasant catches their interest. One thing they rarely do is study the Scriptures with any care. They know nothing of commentaries and reference books. They haven't even a rudimentary knowledge of the principles of hermeneutics or exegesis. As a result, they piece together a strange and inconsistent patchwork of elements derived from these various sources. If you wanted to put together the disorganized, inconsistent, and discordant beliefs of the average Christian in a systematic form, you'd soon find it impossible to do so. The hodge-podge could not be systematized! At best, the result would look like some weak variation of the neo-orthodox paradox in which contradictions predominate!

So, shepherd, what are you going to do about this situation? Are you going to sit passively by watching the church disintegrate even more than it has? Are you going to preside over her demise as a new age of darkness sets in? Or, in those places where you have influence—however pale it may be—are you going to withstand the tide? Are you determined that in one corner of God's pasture, at least, there will be a flock well-informed, able to articulate and defend its faith? Are you going to ward off those forces that would otherwise lead your sheep astray, exposing and opposing them to the hilt? Are you willing to bear up under the criticism that is all but inevitable when you do so? Those are the questions of the day.

CHAPTER 8
DON'T LOSE YOUR REWARD

WHAT does John, the apostle of love, have to say about these matters? Is his approach somewhat more moderate than that of Paul? Judge for yourself.

In his second epistle, John speaks directly to the issue of how a believer is to deal with false teachers. Indeed, the epistle itself is an example of what we have been noticing in Paul's letters. He tells Timothy to *avoid* such persons. John's words to "the elect lady" [which might be translated "the elect Martha"] are totally in sync with those of Paul. His message is to have nothing to do with them lest you help them spread their falsehoods. And, in saying this, John is as plainspoken as Paul. He pulls no punches. In this epistle, in which he stresses love among believers, here is what he also says:

> *Many deceivers have gone out into the world who don't confess that Jesus Christ has come in the flesh;[1] such a person is a deceiver and antichrist.[2] Watch yourselves, that you don't lose that which you have worked for, but rather that you may receive a full reward. Everybody who goes beyond, and doesn't remain in the teaching of Christ, doesn't have God. The one who remains in the teaching has both the Father and the Son. If someone comes to you and doesn't bring this teaching, don't receive him into your home, and don't say "greeting" to him. I say this because the one who says "Greetings" to him shares in his evil deeds (2 John 7-11).*

Say what you will, but if anything, John's words are stronger than Paul's!

---

1   John refers to Gnostics who denied that Jesus had a true human body.
2   That is strong language; it says that the heretic is *against* Christ (*anti* means against).

He says that a heretic is definitely not a Christian. If a man denies the true nature of Jesus Christ, he has neither the Father nor the Son. What shall we say, then, of those who teach "Open Theology"? Do they not deny the true nature of the Father? Should we publish their books, allow them to teach in our schools, or dialogue with them as if we were discussing some fine point about the same God that we both worship? Do true Christians worship and serve a god who doesn't know the future, or One Who knows the end from the beginning? A god who must learn from man rather than predict his future? A god who reacts to man, rather than sovereignly plans and controls the world, His creatures, and all their actions? Judge for yourself!

Now, what else does John say in this small, but all-important epistle? Without a doubt, the object of his pastoral letter is to dissuade the elect Martha from receiving any teachers into her home unless their teaching is strictly orthodox. The problem in 2 John and 3 John that occasioned the two emergency letters was *hospitality*. In the early church, hospitality was an important matter. When Christian missionaries traveled from town to town, often the only place they had to stay was in the homes of believers. In 3 John, the problem was that Diotrophes, an elder in his congregation, refused to receive true missionaries and threw those members out of the church who did. Wanting the preeminence, he refused to share the spotlight with the missionaries. In II John, however, the opposite was true. False teachers were abroad, spreading their beliefs. The question was, "How should we treat *them*?"

John says, refuse to extend hospitality to them; refuse to put them up in your homes. If you do take them in, greeting them as if they were true teachers, you will give them a base of operations from which they may spread their doctrines. And, by doing so, you will be guilty of doing so yourself—just as if you had propagated the falsehoods that they teach (v. 11). The one who assists them in any manner bears the responsibility for doing so. The driver of the getaway car is guilty along with the bank robber!

Here we see how important it is for believers to be able to distinguish true teaching (and teachers) from false teaching (and false teachers). Unless elders instruct the flock in their faith, in the need for discernment and in sniffing out whose teaching is false and why, the members of the flock could never obey directions like those found in 3 John.[3]

The principle that we must not receive or support false teaching can be applied to many other activities today. It applies, for instance, to sending money to radio or TV preachers who set forth false doctrine. It has to do with supporting them by purchasing their materials or attending their conferences for a fee, and so forth. In other words, *nothing* must be done that in any way might further the work of these false teachers. *Surely*, that principle would apply to publishing or selling their books, wouldn't it?

Moreover, John issues a severe warning to those who disobey what he says: "Watch yourselves, that you don't lose that which you have worked for, but rather that you may receive a full reward." In furthering unbelief or erroneous teaching about God, a true believer may lose part of the reward that, otherwise, he might expect to receive for all other good he might have done. If, then, there is even the slightest idea that a teacher's doctrine may be defective so as to fall into a category similar to that of the teachers mentioned by John, the believer ought to beware of assisting him in any way. How many shepherds will lose their reward by aiding and abetting false teachers?[4] A true shepherd will certainly want the full shepherd's reward of which Peter speaks in 1 Peter 5:4.

Moreover, John makes it plain that what to watch out for is teaching that goes "beyond" (v. 9). What does he mean by that? He is speaking of *going beyond* the apostolic teaching (which today is found in the books of the New Testament) that was once for all (*hapax*) deposited with the saints (Jude 3). And, isn't that exactly what we so often find is the problem with heretics and other false teachers—they claim to have "something *more*" to offer!? It is that *appeal to special* (or additional) *knowledge* that the average believer does not possess[5] that allures so many Christians.

---

3   See my book *A Call to Discernment* for help in this matter.
4   Not to combat errorists and their beliefs as John does by writing this epistle also helps them. Failure to stop their inroads into a congregation is nearly as serious as teaching error. This is true, especially when one knows that error is being taught and does nothing about it. And, all of this is most serious in an elder whose office calls him to protect the flock.
5   The problem with the Judaizers was just that; they wanted to *add* circumcision to faith.

They know that their lives are not what they should be. Then, a teacher comes along and asks, "Are you missing something in your Christian life? Well, here is what will fix that for you," and he offers something more, something *beyond*.[6] But the problem is not that he needs something more; usually, what he needs is more of the something he already has.

So 3 John is quite apropos to the issue of this book. While John doesn't present his material in the garb of shepherdly imagery, the principles John enunciated are the same as those we have seen elsewhere clothed with that imagery. New Testament writers were good shepherds—out of love for the sheep they were willing to fight the wolves, and did so! 2 John is an instance of the shepherdly use of the rod and the staff.

---

6   This phraseology almost calls on us to picture a sheep wandering "beyond" the waters of rest and the tender grass!

Chapter 9

Bearding the Lion

To sum up what we have seen thus far, we may say that the elder's task of protecting the flock involves *exposing* and *opposing* error, deception, lying, and falsehood. It is not easy to do this protecting work. We are opposed at every turn by the evil one. Indeed, Satan is pictured in Scripture as "prowling around like a roaring lion, searching for somebody to devour" (1 Peter 5:8). The believer (and, therefore, the elder *par excellence*) is to "Resist him, standing firm in the faith, knowing that" [the] "brotherhood throughout the world fully experiences the same kinds of sufferings" (v. 9).

If this is your task, Christian Elder, then how will you be able to do so? Peter further explains:

> *Now the God of all help, Who has called you to His eternal glory in Christ, after you have suffered a little, will equip, support, strengthen, and firmly establish you (1 Peter 5:10).*

Clearly, the battle will not be easy. You may be wounded in fighting; the enemy may gain victories, and so on. But in the battle, you will not fight alone. When you fight His battles, God, the Source of all true help, is there to "help" (literally "give grace to") you. How does He do so? He lets you "suffer a little," it is true. But in the end, through what you suffer, which only emphasizes your need to turn to Him rather than rely on your own strength, He will equip, support, strengthen, and more firmly establish you in the faith.

In other words, the battle itself will make you stronger and able to do battle more effectively in the future. How does this strengthening, the equipping and the like come? The more we recognize our weaknesses and lack of courage, as we fight for the truth and the One Who is the Truth, the more we find our need for better equipment, more Knowledge, and greater power. So we are driven to the Scriptures, we immerse ourselves in them, and learn so as to be better prepared for future battles. We more earnestly call on God for strength and grow closer to Him all the while. When we have suffered "a little" for our Lord, we have, thereby, more firmly committed ourselves to Him and His church, and so become more solidly established in our faith. In all of this, we can be "more than conquerors" (literally, "more than victors").

But you will not grow by trimming your sails, sidling up to false teachers, or watering down your own doctrine with eclectically gathered teachings. And you will not grow by sitting on the sidelines, allowing the devil to devour sheep after sheep! You will grow only when you are willing to get into the battle, recognizing that, as Peter says, "your opponent" is the devil (v. 8).

God wants good fighters among the elders and the members of His church. That is why in this same verse He commands you to become "level-headed and wide awake." You must be sensible enough to be able to detect the teachings of the wicked one as they are promulgated by his henchmen. That is what God means by being "level-headed." You must have your radar turned on! You must be aware of who is headed in what direction. Moreover, you cannot nap in the tower. Rather, you must ever be "wide awake," alert to every inroad of the devil, not allowing him to get a toehold in your congregation.

Shepherds, as we have seen, have problems with animals. But they also must fight robbers and thieves. Jesus mentioned this in John 10:8 when He said, "All who came before Me are thieves and robbers." He was referring to the false teachers who preceded Him, claiming that they were the Messiah. In his book *The Perfect Shepherd*, John Davis wrote:

> One of the real dangers to the shepherd and his flocks is the thief who has roamed the rugged hills of Palestine from the most ancient of times. Mohammed Yaseen remarked a number of times that the thief is one of his great fears. The shepherd is very vulnerable because of the deep wadis and passes through which he must go. Raids on flocks of sheep and goats are still common in the eastern deserts of Jordan. Often this leads to open warfare between various nomadic groups.[1]

---

1   *Op. cit.*, p. 47.

Today there are also cultists and others who make grandiose claims.[2] For instance, one group with growing influence, People of Destiny International (PDI), speaks of "gift ministries" given to the church by God, "that it might mature and grow."[3] So far, so good. But these, they say, include apostles and prophets, which are necessary to nurture and equip "all members of the church … for the work of ministry." Certainly, there were apostles and prophets (separated by Paul from the other ministry gifts in Ephesians 2:20 and 3:5 as *foundational ministries through which revelation would be given*, not as perpetual gifts). But does PDI teach true Christian doctrine when it boasts present-day prophets and apostles? The claim is that they "employ apostolic oversight to identify and raise up indigenous leaders able to build strong local churches." How can they claim apostolic authority in the light of the fact that to be an apostle one must have seen Jesus (1 Corinthians 9:1)?[4] One can only think of Revelation 2:2, where Jesus commends the church at Ephesus because they have "tested those who call themselves apostles, and aren't, and found them liars."

This group also, through the music that it disseminates, has begun to gain a large, uncritical following. It is the task of true shepherds to warn and expose the body of churches that is being raised up under this PDI name for what it is. The danger is that they represent themselves as thorough-going evangelicals. In their statement of faith, they claim that "there is nothing new here." But apostles appearing in our day—can we simply take that as a minor difference of belief? Read again Revelation 2:2!

PDI claims not to "change" the Scriptures by "extra-biblical revelation." Does that mean it is satisfactory to claim such revelation so long as it is not in conflict with the Bible? If, in some "Grudem-esque" fashion, they lay claim to prophecy that is not revelatory, then (as one must also ask Wayne Grudem) why have prophets and prophecy at all? And, how can there be divinely inspired prophecy that is not revelatory? Every word

---

2   See my comments about this matter in *Signs and Wonders in the Last Days.*
3   PDI is now known as Sovereign Grace Ministries, based in Gaithersburg, Maryland. The teaching is from PDI's web site, www.pdinet.org/about/faith.html.
4   Would there be claims that this has happened?

from God is inspired, inerrant, and adds something to our understanding of Him and His will. If it does not, it fails to serve its purpose.

In addition to the errors just mentioned, the teaching of the group is that "all the gifts of the Holy Spirit at work in the church of the first century are available today." That means they claim to be able to raise the dead, heal miraculously, and so on. In addition, they believe in the old Pentecostal doctrine of a second work of grace, which they say is a "theologically distinct" experience from being indwelled by the Spirit, and "subsequent to conversion as well." Of course, there are all of the problems with that sort of teaching that the church has encountered for many years.

Elder, are you aware of this emerging group and others similar to it? Are you able and willing to withstand their influence upon your congregation should that become a problem? Do you even know what inroads they may have made already—or soon might seek to make? In other words, do you keep up with what is going on around you? Evidently the apostles did, and they did something about it whenever they spotted a problem. They were true shepherds!

CHAPTER 10

PLAYING FOOTSIES WITH ROME

CHARLES COLSON has created a problem that the evangelical churches did not need. His influence following his conversion and entrance into the life of the church has exerted more than enough pressure upon Bible-believing churches to consider detente with Rome. In his November 4, 1994, article in *Christianity Today* entitled "Why Catholics are our Allies," Colson calls Roman Catholicism nothing more than a "distinctive theological tradition."[1] He wants us to become (as Schaeffer put it) "co-belligerents" with Rome on such issues as "abortion, pornography, and threats to religious liberty." He sees Christians and Roman Catholics as holding to but one faith in two distinctive bodies. He believes that we simply disagree upon many non-essentials but, nevertheless, are united in the essentials: Romanists and evangelicals alike are Christians. Therefore, he calls for a working union of *Evangelicals and Catholics Together*[2] (ECT).

Rome has never changed her basic beliefs. She still thinks she is the only true church, and (despite the statement of various liberal theologians within Romanism) believes that there is no salvation outside of the church. Rome has not repudiated the most serious error she teaches—that the death of Jesus Christ on the cross was insufficient for the salvation of God's elect. Rather, she still boasts of the mass in which Christ is said to be sacrificed daily in an unbloody death on thousands of altars all over the world. The "one sacrifice ... forever" (Hebrews 10:12) of which the New Testament speaks is thereby repudiated.

Ceremonies and works form the structure of the Romanist faith. The Council of Trent anathematized the truth of justification by faith alone, thereby turning what was already a fact into a doctrinal reality: Rome became a cult. She is the largest cult, but nevertheless a cult after all. All

---

1   p. 136.
2   The name of his organization.

that the Reformers suffered for in order to shake off the shackles of Rome is presently at stake. Because of the new rapprochement, in recent times a number of so-called evangelicals have gone over to Romanism. And there are many more who are, at least, willing to "play footsies" with her. Those who have signed the ECT statement have indicated their willingness to do so, and by doing so have weakened the biblical wall that the reformers erected between Roman heresy and biblical truth.

Every elder-shepherd must watch out for the Roman wolf that wants to lure dissenting, Protestant sheep back into her fold. But Romanism is no sheepfold in which weary sheep may find safety, certainty, and rest; it is a place of uncertainty, despair, and spiritual death for all who enter it by faith. The faith of Rome offers partial salvation by Christ, to which is added works-righteousness and ceremonies to take up the slack! Because men like Colson and J. I. Packer have become a part of ECT, many in the church are confused. They must be informed that, fundamentally, Rome hasn't changed since the days of Luther and Calvin. And, because that is true, the reasons for keeping a large distance from her have not changed either.

It is this slipping away from our Protestant forefathers' firm stand for the truth of the Scriptures that is so obvious in the recent buddying up to Rome. It becomes only one more reason to be on the alert for future inroads by people who wish to see early contacts grow into a more substantive relationship—leading to eventual absorption.

The reformers used the language of the apostle John when speaking of Rome as "antichrist." Were they wrong? Or has the pluralism of our day so eroded the truth that even those who ought to know better do not? Whatever the reason or reasons may be, in the eyes of many, Rome looks attractive. But then again, the phenomenon of a wolf in sheep's clothing, and the revealed fact that Satan's emissaries come to God's people as "apostles" while he masquerades as an "angel of light" (2 Corinthians 11:13, 14) must be borne in mind.

This idea of co-belligerency has led to the weakening of the wall of separation between Rome and the true church. Sure, there are plenty of secular foes who need to be withstood. But the idea of gathering together with the Mormons, the Muslims, Rome, and whoever else may agree with us on some issues is a devastatingly wrong one that, if vigorously pursued, will lead to all sorts of colossal compromises that dwarf present ones. It is like siding with a wolf against a bear!

We stand with God, not with heretics, against our enemies. It was when Israel went down to Egypt or appealed to Assyria for help in fighting common foes that she apostatized from God. We do not need the support of unbelievers and cultists in order to maintain our faith.[3] Our God can supply everything necessary. But even so, better that members of the church be persecuted than to run to Rome for support.

It is important to note that Scripture describes the common practice of true shepherds banding together to withstand a lion (Isaiah 31:4). How important it is to foster unity among true Christians! Instead of fighting one another and uniting with cultists, heretics, and unbelievers, we must learn to work together to defend our flocks. And it is from just such groups as we have been encouraged to unite with that we must defend them.

Colson is quite wrong when, in his article, he calls "all orthodox believers to unite on the great truth of the faith against secular modernism and theological liberalism." It is precisely the *great* issues of our faith that keep us from uniting with Rome. She denies them. When he says that "our best weapon is the distinctiveness of Christian truth, expressed in unity by all believers," he downplays the crucial fact that it is about the "distinctiveness of Christian truth" that the reformers separated from Rome. These distinctives were buried under centuries of tradition and heretical teaching so that they could no longer be found. The reformers cracked off Romish barnacles and returned to the truths that for so long had been hidden and distorted.

Shepherds, aware of this tendency of some to draw close to Rome once again, will want to warn their sheep about the problems that arise in doing so. How can believers stand side-by-side with those who, in numerous ways, deny the once-for-all death of Jesus Christ for the

3   That is not to say that God, in His providence, may not use Rome or others to help the church combat forces that would destroy religion. But it is one thing for God to use Cyrus as His servant and another for the church to call upon Cyrus to render service to her (cf. Isaiah 44:28).

redemption of guilty sinners? Any Roman Catholic who believes the doctrines of Rome is lost.[4] Rome does not teach the biblical way of salvation. As a shepherd of Christ's flock, then, you must oppose Rome and do all you can to keep your sheep from her grasp.

---

4   That is not to say that within the Roman church there are not true believers who, in one way or another, have come to a knowledge of the truth. But they are few in number and are saved not *because* of the teaching they received from Rome, but *in spite of* it.

CHAPTER 11
USING THE STAFF WITH THE DISTAFF

That there are those within the evangelical church today who advocate feminism is one of the saddest (and clearest) evidences of the erosion of biblical faith due to modern cultural impact. It has gone so far that "Christian" publishing houses are now helping destroy the English language by enforcing gender neutral words and phrases. Such grammatically horrendous constructions as "Each one must think about their responsibility" are found everywhere today. Clearly, *each one* and *their* do not correspond. But we see this kind of thing appearing all over, simply in order to avoid saying such things as "Each one must think about *his* responsibility." The "his" already is neutral in such sentences, but those who want to promote feminism are bent on eliminating it, since (obviously) the word "his" also has a masculine reference.

That Christian publishing companies have yielded to such nonsense plainly evidences the extent to which contemporary cultural influences have made inroads into the Church. Elder-shepherds ought to resist all such foolish concessions to that influence by urging their flock to recognize what is happening and refusing to purchase volumes that give credence to neutralizing the language by destroying it.

Not only have books been "sanitized" so as not to use the hated word "his," but even the Bible itself has been tampered with. Consider the following verses taken at random from the *New Revised Standard Version* (NRSV):

For you were called to freedom, brothers and sisters ... (Galatians 5:13)

My friends, if anyone is detected in a transgression ... (Galatians 6:1)

The original Greek of Galatians 5:13 is "brothers," not "brothers and sisters." The words "and sisters" are simply added! In Galatians 6:1, the

Greek also reads "brothers," not "My friends." What liberties are taken with the Word of God!

To "correct" the Scriptures in such a fashion, so as to conform to feminist ideology (and this sort of thing will be found throughout the NRSV) is not only presumptuous, but it is also dangerous. Remember the Lord's words of warning: "To all who hear the words of the prophecy of this scroll I testify this: If anybody adds to them God will add to him the plagues that are written in this scroll" (Revelation 22:18). And, seemingly heedless of the warning,[5] the very next verse in the NRSV reads "*that person's* share" in which "that person's" is substituted for the Greek "*his* part." This problem is not only a difficulty with the NRSV; more "conservative" versions have also been affected.

Of course, in addition, the pressure has been rising from feminists within the evangelical church to ordain women as elders the way that the mainline liberal denominations do. To do so, however, is a direct violation of such passages as 1 Timothy 2:12: "I don't permit a woman to teach or exercise authority over a man but to remain silent." As we have seen earlier in this book, the basic function of all elders is to rule ("exercise authority over"). An additional function of some elders is to teach. It is perfectly plain, therefore, that by these words Paul was forbidding the ordination of women to the eldership.

"But that was a cultural thing," someone insists. As a matter of fact, it wasn't. Paul cites two bases for his decision: creation and the fall (v. 13, 14). No two events in world history were less culturally conditioned! God and the garden, along with man in his perfect state prior to the fall, constituted the only culture involved.

There is, then, every sort of specious argument raised to justify the ordination of women. For instance, Galatians 3:28 is torn from its context in order to do service to the feminist cause. It reads, "There is neither Jew nor Greek, there is neither slave nor free, there is neither male nor female; you are all one in Christ Jesus." The passage does not say that gender is eliminated with reference to office. The passage has nothing to say about office. Paul is talking about how one is saved. All are equal

---

5   Or, anxious to thrust the wording "in one's face."

before God, regardless of race, social status, or gender, when it comes to becoming "God's sons" (v. 26).[6] Such desperate attempts on the part of "evangelical" feminists ought to be abandoned. They should be honest enough to recognize what the Bible teaches and submit to it—or admit that they simply do not accept it. In this respect, the liberals are much more forthright.

Not only are there women preachers in the mainline liberal churches, but the same phenomenon has been found in the Pentecostal, Holiness, and black churches for years. This failure to follow biblical teachings has passed over into a number of the charismatic congregations of our day. Their influence, in many ways, including influence in this matter, has more and more affected the evangelical church.

Shepherds, you must hold the line—or, where it has already sagged, reestablish the line—against all the intrusion of feminist thinking that has weakened the church and misrepresented the Word of God. It is not that Christian leaders are anti-women; nothing could be farther from the truth. One glimpse at the favorable mention of women in the letters of Paul (who is often vilified by feminists as a woman-hating bachelor) is all that is necessary to dispel such notions. Not only is such talk a calumny against God, it is an attack on the inspiration of Scripture. The problem Bible-believing shepherds have is not with women; it is with women who want to break down the barrier between men and women in the eldership and other role relationships that God Himself established.

So, then, there is much to be done to stem the onrushing tide of feminism in the church. And it is up to elder-shepherds to reign in straying sheep who, in disregard for the Scriptures, are turning each one to his (should I have said "her?") own way. Elder, has feminism crept into your congregation? If so, what are you doing to counteract it? Anything?

---

6   The NRSV typically distorts the Greek by substituting "children of God" for "sons."

CHAPTER 12

CONFRONTING THE MYSTIC WOLF

THE word "mystic" comes from the Greek word *muo*, which means "closed." It referred to closing the lips in order to keep a secret. The mystery religions, for instance, were closed or secret religions into which one had to be initiated.

The mystic claims to have an ineffable experience with God that results from becoming one with Him in some sense or other (note the word "experience"; it's a good summary term for everything involved in mysticism). Mystics speak of merging with or into God. This supposed experience, being ineffable, of course, cannot be explained. Winfried Corduan of Taylor University, who is a modern proponent of mysticism, in his book *Mysticism: An Evangelical Option?* says, "After all, mysticism is a phenomenon of many dimensions."[1] This is true, but all he is acknowledging is the fact of its vagueness. He is unable to nail it down. Since what Corduan says is true, no two authors can agree on a definition. Carl Keller, in *Mysticism and Philosophical Analysis*, wrote, "it is a word devoid of concrete meaning."[2] The mystic will say, "You can understand it only when you experience it."

Typically, mysticism bypasses the Bible. At best, it is another attempt to obtain "something more."[3] But, ordinarily, it is a substitute even for the "something" that all Christians have as the result of their salvation in Christ. The mystic search is driven by dissatisfaction. The mystic is impatient; progressive sanctification is too slow. He wants what he wants NOW. The experience supposedly is reached through a series of steps, which vary with the particular mystical system one follows.[4]

---

1   Zondervan (1991), p. 11.
2   Oxford (1978), p. 96. For a further study of this see Jay E. Adams, *Ending the Quest for Something More.*
3   This additional *something* may be blessedness, truth, enlightenment or holiness obtained by means of an *unmediated* (direct) encounter with God.
4   Such as purgation, illumination, union.

The Bible knows nothing of a mystical experience. It has largely been the fruit of monasticism and other Roman Catholic devotions, though there have always been people within so-called Protestantism who have advocated it. Monastics, and others who remain awake an inordinate number of hours, may have experiences that they misinterpret as absorption into the Infinite (or whatever), that are actually caused by sleep loss. In many people, significant sleep loss can lead to all the effects of LSD.

Whenever a shepherd learns of a sheep who has "turned to his own way" by attempting some mystic approach to God, he must warn him of the error of this way. Taking the staff and gently rescuing him from falling from the mystical precipice, he will inform him of the unbiblical nature of what he is up to. But he will not stop there. He will counsel him to see what it was that made him think he needed something more (or something other) than what he has in sanctification, which is the biblical means of growing to be more like Christ. In almost every case, when a believer is dissatisfied with the ordinary means of spiritual growth that is found in Scripture, it is because he has sin in his life to which he has fallen prey. Either he finds that its grasp is stronger than he has been able to break or that he doesn't know what to do to escape from it. The shepherd-counselor will work with him at conquering his sin through repentance, leading to the biblical put off/put on dynamic found in Ephesians 4; Colossians 3, and elsewhere.[5]

A form of mysticism is often connected with faith healing and other "charismatic" activities. Those who promote these experience-driven activities encourage followers to "feel" and "experience" the presence of God. Since God is a Spirit and has no tangible aspect to His being, it is impossible to feel or sense His presence. In order to do so, the one who wants the "experience" must churn up some sort of feeling that he may interpret as the "presence" or "power" of God.

It is important to understand feelings so that we do not misjudge them. Though much is said about them in modern religions of various sorts, it is not a Christian objective to achieve certain feelings. That the

5   To understand and apply this dynamic, consult *The Christian Counselor's Manual.*

Christian may feel sad, joyful, happy, upset, peaceful, and so on, of course, is true. God gave us all feelings, and every feeling is right in its place (that place being the one that is biblically appropriate). But these feelings are our perception of our bodily states every bit as much as when we say, "I'm tired; I'm sick." The feelings that we feel arise from bodily conditions, which, in turn, arise from thoughts, expectations, conscience, and so on. In other words, we do not feel *God*, but because of our thinking, we feel bodily emotional states that we interpret as happy, peaceful, or (wrongly) as God's presence.

Mysticism has been described as "mindless religion." That is not a bad description. Understood as such, it can be seen to be in direct violation of 1 Corinthians 14:14 and 15, where the entire emphasis in our worship is upon conscious, clear, mental activity.

Mysticism is caught up in producing certain states that it claims are in such close relationship to God that it is often impossible to say what is God and what is human in the experience, as the two are merged. The line between the creature and his Creator is blurred—or even erased. That very concept is a type of pantheistic heresy since God and a sinful human being cannot come into contact in such a way. "No one comes to the Father," Jesus said, "except by Me." Yet, the mystic is quite ready to attempt to reach God in other ways than through Christ and the gospel.

Because of the mystic's unique experience and gnostic-like knowledge, he may assume an air of superiority over the rest of us peons. Madam Guyon, for instance, spoke of writing her books for the few who, with her, practiced what she called "interior prayer." The one with ultra-truth gleaned from an ultra-experience of becoming one with God can easily think of himself as a super saint!

All of this accords perfectly with a fundamental self-centeredness that lies at the heart of the mystic. His emphasis is upon the first great commandment at the expense of the second. Mystics are principally concerned about themselves—their experience of God. Consequently, by ignoring the second great commandment, they deceive themselves into thinking that they have attained the first when, the truth is, they know little of either.

One of the giveaways that exposes mysticism as unchristian is the fact that Muslims, Hindus, and others who do not know the true God and who reject Jesus Christ as Savior also report experiences that parallel those of the "Christian" mystics.[6] Obviously, since they believe in a god other than the God and Father of Jesus Christ, and since John says that no one has the Father unless he has the Son, these experiences are contrived—just as are those of the "Christian" mystic. It is possible for true Christians to stray into mysticism, just as a sheep may stray into paths other than those in which the shepherd wants to lead him. But it is not possible to become a Christian by taking the mystic route since it bypasses salvation through Christ.

---

6   Modern Yoga (from the Sanskrit, "to yoke, join, unite") consists of bodily exercises designed to reach a point of union with Brahma ("the infinite"). Jewish mystics seek *devekuth*, which means "adherence to" or "clinging to" God.

CHAPTER 13

DENYING SUFFICIENCY

O VER the years, I have written and said enough about the tendency of many supposed Bible-believing people to eclectically add psychological and psychiatric concepts and methods to the biblical data in the area of counseling. Paul wrote that the Bible is sufficient for "the man from God"[1] and that all he would ever need to carry on his work for God successfully would be found in it. In three different ways he said that the Scriptures are sufficient; he said that they were God-breathed 1) "in order to make the man from God adequate," and 2) "to equip him fully" 3) "for every good task" (2 Timothy 3:17). The Scriptures will make him "adequate" for the work of changing people God's way;[2] they will "fully equip him" to meet the exigencies that arise and by means of biblical truth he will be able to handle "every good task" to which God calls him. How could he have said it more clearly or more fully? To be true to their calling, shepherds must take a stand. After all, Psalm 23:1 says that God supplies everything that His sheep need: that is to say they "shall not lack."

What is true of counseling is also true in other areas as well. It applies to every task of shepherding. In our time, all too often, the evangelical church has ignored this divine pronouncement and, instead, has turned elsewhere for direction. For instance, churches have borrowed all sorts of gimmicks and strategies from the business world to support their church growth efforts. But the church is not a business. Business exists to make profits; the flock must be cared for even at the sacrifice of profits. There is an entirely different ethos behind each. But in this area, as in others, God's shepherdly provisions have been ignored.

The book of Acts, together with the epistles, clearly shows how to grow churches; there is no need to look elsewhere for help. Biblical sufficiency,

---

1   A phrase picked up from the Old Testament and applied in the New to the shepherd-elder.
2   For details, see my book *How to Help People Change*.

as a theological doctrine, seems to be unknown to many. Shepherds have a lot of work to do in indoctrinating the church about this matter. Perhaps they will best be able to do this by demonstrating it in their own ministries. It is the task of those who shepherd God's flock not only to discover all that He has provided in Scriptures to carry out their tasks, but to instruct the churches where they serve how to appropriate all that He has made available—"… His divine power has given us everything for life and godliness …" (2 Peter 1:3, 4).

Frequently, doctrine has been taught abstractly without showing how it is relevant to life. And even when its relevance is shown, too often little or nothing has been shown about how to turn doctrine into life. True, the *what to* is missing, but much more frequently, the *how to* is totally absent. Consequently, people do not know how to appropriate truth into daily living. Shepherds must guide them in this matter. In Titus 1:1, Paul explains that truth is important because it is intended to lead to godliness. That truth must be sounded throughout the church, and shepherds everywhere must see to it that the transformation of truth into godliness takes place.

But something must also be said about other extra-biblical revelatory emphases that seem to be growing in many churches. When biblical sufficiency is denied in practice, people will find something else to take its place. Other emphases abound. These emphases take many different forms. A pervasive one is the idea that God will guide us in ways *apart from* the Bible. I have dealt with this false belief in a book called *The Christian's Guide to Guidance*. In it, I have shown that the Bible nowhere encourages us to turn to dreams, hunches, sensations, feelings, providential circumstances, promptings, checks in the spirit, leadings, and the like. All of these manmade formulae for discerning God's will bypass the Bible and indicate that those who follow them may say one thing, but actually think that the Scriptures are *not sufficient* for knowing His will. Now, when God says otherwise, it is serious business on the one hand to affirm that the Bible is sufficient, and on the other hand, in one's practice, act as if it were not. Every time a shepherd turns to outside help, he leads the sheep astray.

It is the elder-shepherd's work to carefully study and exposit the Scriptures for the sheep so that they will recognize that there is all that they could need for Christian living in the Scriptures. They must see that because of the faithful shepherd's teaching, counsel, and guidance, they "do not lack." That, perhaps, is one of the greatest needs in the church today—shepherd-teachers who feed the flock adequately. It is because there are so few teachers who spend the time and make the effort to guide the flock to the green tender grasses of the Bible that they soon become prey to wolves in shepherd's clothing who tempt them with offers of greener pastures. A well-fed sheep is not as likely to wander from the flock.

If shepherds were doing their job of properly teaching and counseling the members of their flocks, not only would they have less need to wander elsewhere for sustenance, but the shepherds would have less reason to use the rod and the staff. As it is, today, sheep are scattered, wandering all over the place in search of solid food. More often than not, however, they find themselves entering pastures and sheepfolds of the enemy.

There is a need for church discipline[3] when sheep fail to remain in the flock. Not only should the shepherd of his sheep be willing to exercise discipline when it is necessary to do so in order to reclaim lost, straying sheep, but each shepherd must be willing to lead wandering sheep back to their shepherds.[4] That means that they should be willing to counsel sheep who stray into their congregations from another biblical one about returning to their flocks. Often, such "church hoppers" need to go back and face certain persons with whom they have had difficulties. The answer is not to "run" from the problem to some other church. They must truly "solve" their problems. The pastor who accepts sheep who come from a different sheepfold for illegitimate reasons—to change the figure—is taking a Jonah into his boat. He will soon experience the waves that follow, and, in the end, he will have to throw him overboard! They may not think so, but under such conditions, they are getting no bargain when they take them into membership.

All in all, it may be confidently said that sheep will always stray because they still sin—no matter how good the shepherd may be. But there will be less straying where the Word of God is recognized as sufficient,

---

3   See my *Handbook of Church Discipline.*
4   That is, when the sheep belong to a true shepherd. not to a false or wicked one.

and where faithful shepherding is practiced. The staff of discipline will have to be practiced less frequently, and the flock will have rest.

CHAPTER 14

PROPER SHEPHERDING PRECLUDES PROBLEMS

PETER was the man who forgot. Jesus told him that he would deny Him three times before the cock crowed. After the third denial, the cock crowed, their eyes met, and Peter remembered! Then, too late, he went out and wept bitterly. Every Sunday School child knows the sad story. Yet, that isn't the end. Following the resurrection, Peter must have thought he was finished as an apostle because he had gone back to work, fishing. Jesus met him at the sea, revealed Himself, and restored Peter to the apostleship (John 21:15-19). The restoration was complete: as there were three denials, so there were three restorations. Significantly, each of these was a restoration to *shepherding*, indicating that apostleship essentially involved a shepherding ministry.

Jesus planned this three-fold recall to apostleship in a way that met all aspects of the denials. Peter had denied Jesus around a charcoal fire; he was restored around a charcoal fire.[1] Peter had boasted that if all others forsook Him, he would not do so. Referring to this fact, Jesus asked him, "Do you love Me more than these [the rest of the disciples]?" (John 21:15). The re-created elements of this restoration, recalling the three failures, were not intended to "rub it in," but, rather, were gracious, designed to indicate that nothing more needed to be done; all the negative elements of Peter's denials had been taken into consideration and dealt with—definitively!

One other feature, missed in the King James version, is the use of the word "love" in verses 15 through 17. Christ asks, "Do you *love* Me?" Peter responds, "Yes, Lord, You know I *care* for You" (v. 15). Jesus asks again, "Do you *love* Me?" (v. 16). Once more Peter responds, "You know I *care* for You" (v. 16). Finally Jesus asks, "Simon ... do you *care* for Me?" (v. 17). At that change from *love* to *care for*, Peter was upset (literally,

---

1   The KJV fails to bring out this significant feature.

"deeply hurt"), and so not knowing how to respond, he threw it all back on Jesus: "Lord, You know all things; You know that I love You." Three times Peter denied Him. Now three times, ending in a clear expression of Jesus' deity, Peter reaffirms his loving faith and commitment to Christ.

Jesus used shepherdly language in restoring Peter. Here is what He said:

1. "Feed My lambs," giving Peter a charge to teach the young, children of the flock.
2. "Shepherd My sheep," charging Peter to care for and rule over the adult members of the flock.
3. "Feed My sheep," laying a charge on Peter to teach adults as well.

The call to "shepherding" of the sheep restored Peter to the elder's ruling and managing function, while "feeding" restored him to the work of teaching as well. Both aspects of the eldership (which Peter acknowledged as his calling in 1 Peter 5:1) were thus conferred upon the repentant apostle.

Peter, himself, explains what this shepherdly work involved in 1 Peter 5:1 through 4. Using Jesus' own words, he exhorts "fellow-elders" to "shepherd the flock among you" (v. 2). He then adds in explanation, "exercising oversight" (i.e., acting as a bishop[2]). Plainly, in Peter's mind, the command to "shepherd the flock" meant to function as a bishop (or ruling elder) to whom the flock had been entrusted. Their safety was his obligation.

In his follow-up letter, Peter—the man who forgot—does all he can to encourage the elders to whom he was writing not to forget what he was telling them. He is concerned about precluding problems that he knew might otherwise occur. Accordingly, he "reminds" them, by way of warning, about false teachers who would come, seeking entrance into the sheepfold. He wrote,

> *But there were false prophets among the people just as there will be false teachers among you, who secretly will bring in destructive, divi-*

---

2   One who "oversees" as a superintendent.

sive dogmas, even denying the Master Who bought them,³ bringing swift destruction upon themselves. Many will follow their immoral ways, and because of them the true Way will be maligned. Because of greed they will get money out of you with their fabricated stories. Their long-standing judgment doesn't linger and their destruction doesn't slumber (1 Peter 2:1-3).

Then, in strong words of warning, Peter cites the judgment of Noah's day and the destruction of Sodom and Gomorrah as evidence of how God deals with such people, while sparing believers (2:4-22).

In 2 Peter 3:1 and following, Peter repeats the fact that he is reminding them of that which they knew full well because he had taught them previously about these teachers. He even discusses the type of charges (or complaints) that the heretics would level against the doctrine of the second coming and instructs them how to respond to these (3:3-13).

Peter concludes with an exhortation about how Paul's letters are being misconstrued by "unstable and untaught" persons (v. 15, 16), of whom he wrote earlier (2:17-19):

These persons are waterless springs and fogs driven by a hurricane, for whom the gloomy darkness has been reserved. Through uttering impressive-sounding claptrap, by an appeal to fleshly desires and to impure practices, they bait a trap for persons who have already escaped from those who live in error, promising them freedom while they themselves are slaves of corruption (one is a slave of whatever has defeated him).

Once again, we encounter the admonition to "guard." Here, he sees elders, as well as members, possibly being carried away by the errors of "lawless persons" who would cause them to fall (v. 17).

In all of this, consider several things:

1. There is a need to *remind* elders about false teachers and the threat they pose to the flocks that they oversee. Reminding

---

3   Who denied? The "people" of Israel, who, as a people, had been "bought" by the Lord.

      people is one way to preclude problems. That, therefore, is a major purpose of the book that you hold in your hands.

2.   Protecting the flock from error is principally the work of elders. As a restored elder, Peter considered it his duty to warn fellow elders not to forget this work of protecting the sheep from error.

3.   The recipients of Peter's letter—even those in charge—are to "guard" themselves so as not to be deceived by those who would carry them away from the faith (3:17). Elders, too, can be duped. Indeed, that is one of the major problems in the church today!

4.   Once more, Peter uses very strong language to describe the heretics (read the letter through out loud, placing the proper emphasis upon the passages that do so). He is not mild and timid; he "tells it like it is." So should you; this is serious business, not to be handled gently.

5.   Peter speaks of the "heresies" that these false teachers promulgate not as "alternative viewpoints" but as destructive, divisive dogmas.

6.   He says that these teachings will be introduced *secretly*. That means that elders must be even more alert than they might be otherwise.

7.   He sets the Lord squarely against the teachers and their teachings. Unless the elders of the church take their stand alongside their Lord in this matter, they will be found opposing Him!

Elders must do as Peter exhorts, or havoc will occur in their churches. Those who listen to Jesus, Peter, and the other apostles and properly protect their flocks will, by doing so, prevent many difficulties.

All elders ought to read Peter's two epistles at least once every quarter in their elders' meetings as the reminders they were intended to be. It is important to know—as we shall see later in this book—that Peter's words were no more heeded than were Christ's when He warned him about denying Him three times. Some people learn only when it is too late—the hard way. Is that the way you want to learn? Must your congregation be placed in jeopardy because you forget the multitude of warnings about false teachers in the Bible? Why not listen to Peter and the rest, and guard your flock, which, remember, is not yours but God's?

Another way to prevent problems through proper shepherding is to become so close to the sheep that you know them well and they know you and your voice. When that sort of closeness prevails, the situation that Jesus described also will prevail: "his sheep follow him [the good shepherd] because they know his voice" (John 10:4). And, in turn, "they certainly won't follow a stranger; rather, they will flee from him because they don't know the voice of strangers" (John 10:5). That is what you want—a flock that will not follow the teaching of others who teach differently.

How is it that a shepherd may gain such "closeness" to the sheep? The biblical shepherd spent most of his waking hours (and sleeping time as well) out with his sheep. They walked together, they heard him speak their names, they felt his healing touch, and they enjoyed his companionship. The same must be true of spiritual shepherds.

If a shepherd of the sheep spends time with his flock, doing things with them, caring for and guiding them, they will come to appreciate it, and will not readily depart from the fold. If he is with them in times of need and heartache, ministering the healing Word to them, they will find it difficult to follow the word of another. If he has counseled them through hard family times, been with them in times of sickness and death, ministered to them when perplexed, they will hear his voice—and not another's. If he has nourished them on fresh teaching from the Scriptures, grown and harvested at great effort, they will find it hard to stray from such strengthening food. Nothing more than care and feeding of the flock, then, can prevent the sheep from wandering away from the truth. But while these aspects of shepherding are critical, when the wolf comes, the shepherd must also stand between it and the sheep.

CHAPTER 15

HOW THE WOLF CREEPS IN

ORDINARILY, error doesn't come galloping in on a sweaty steed announcing itself for what it is; it crawls, creeps, and insinuates itself. Jude wrote of "certain persons" who "have slipped in surreptitiously" (Jude 4). When I read those words, I think of the proverbial boys sneaking into the circus tent by lifting up a flap and crawling in unobserved. The analogy is close to the entry of Jude's errorists. They come in when people are unaware of what they are and why they have come.

I have already noted what Paul said about Satan appearing as an "apostle" and his minions deceptively disguised coming into churches as "angels [messengers] of Light." That means, of course, that they come with some supposedly important and uplifting "truth" ("light") that the church (they say) has neglected to teach or has misunderstood. They will often appear as those who are committed to the Bible, who are thoroughly conservative and interested only in helping poor, benighted church members who have been under the oppressive hand of foolish elder-shepherds. Sadly, they will have little difficulty uncovering reasons to say such things about the eldership of many a church today. That, naturally, gives them a ready entrance into it to propagate their heresies.

People succumb to error incrementally. Psalm 1 makes this clear. First, they are attracted to and "walk" toward (into) the "way of the wicked." At this point, they have no intention of becoming involved. But then, as they linger, listening to the counsel of the wicked, they become interested. They stop, and "stand in the path of sinners." Finally, they become a part of the wickedness itself, even enlisting others: they "sit in the seat of mockers." The seat is the place of instruction of others.

This progress of Christians into evil ways is, therefore, usually not all at once, as you can see. Nor is it even obvious at the outset. It happens in stages, which elder-shepherds must be wise enough to detect. When they are able to do so, they can cut it off at the pass! Frequently, however, the elders move in (if at all) only when most of the damage has been done;[1] the person has reached stage three as set forth in the Psalm. Elders must learn to spot problems early on and warn and instruct those who are becoming enamored with error to turn away before it is too late, when they too have become "scorners, mockers" of the truth.

Jude recognized that what Peter warned about in his second letter was actually happening in the church to which he wrote[2]—the false teachers had gotten more than a toehold in it. So, he wrote this entire letter in terms of Peter's in order to urge the church to "contend vigorously for the faith that was delivered to the saints in a full and final way" (v. 3). There are important facts to note here.

First, Jude says that the false teachers had been allowed to move in; that means that the elders had not been as vigilant as they should have been (Acts 20:31). That is the problem to which this book is addressed. The history of the church, with all of its heresy and schisms, is a history of elder failure. If you do not understand that and respond accordingly, then I have written in vain.

Second, though Peter had previously warned them about the problem before it became so serious, they had failed to listen to his warning. That is the situation in many congregations today; elders and their sheep have failed to listen to God's warnings and, consequently, have taken no action to guard against enemies of their flocks. This fact shows plainly that Jude's words are applicable.

Third, now belatedly, they had to "contend for their faith." That sounds like urging a shepherd who has allowed the wolf into the sheepfold, and now, only after the wolf has hold of a sheep, to do something about it. Verses 22 and 23 show that the wolf had created serious problems among the members of the flock. Some had already been devoured by wolfish error, others were on the way to becoming a part of it, and still

---

1   In the next chapter, we shall see how this happened in the church to which Jude wrote.
2   It was probably the same church which had failed to heed Peter's warning. That may be why Jude writes in the present tense virtually what Peter wrote in the future tense.

others were wondering about the error. How much better if the shepherd had kept him out in the first place!

Fourth, they must contend for the faith. They were not to go out picking a fight; they were to defend the flock from error by guarding and maintaining the true faith. The battle had been taken to them; the enemy was in their territory and doing much harm. They must take up the rod and begin to use it.

Fifth, the faith in question had been delivered to the saints once-for-all (*hapax*). There was no "new" or "different" revelation to come.[3] That faith is the "deposit" of truth that was delivered to the apostles who, in turn, handed it over to the church at large. It was not to be added to or subtracted from. Rather, it was to be preserved and passed on intact.

> *Timothy, guard that which was entrusted to you, turning away from the irreligious chatter and contradictions of what is falsely labeled "knowledge," which some have professed but by taking poor aim have missed the target of the faith (1 Timothy 6:20, 21; see also 2 Timothy 1:13, 14; 2:2).*

False teachers always come with "something else, something new, or something different." Elders must always be on the lookout for those who use such language or offer such messages. According to Mark 13:5, elders, too, may be misled.

Sixth, Jude urges a "vigorous" defense of the faith. How little of that is seen in congregations today! If any appears at all, usually it is too late, too restrained, and too weak. Only a deep love for the sheep will impel shepherds to contend vigorously against wolves and lions who would devour them. The picture that comes to mind is that of a shepherd plunging headlong into the fray to deliver his sheep from a wild animal.

---

3   See also John 16:13. Jesus told the disciples that when the Spirit would come, He would lead them (the apostles) into *all truth*. No more truth was to be expected beyond what the apostles taught and recorded in the books of the New Testament. In 1 John 4:6, when discussing how to distinguish those who teach error from those who teach truth, John makes it plain that those who listen to the truth taught by the apostles are true teachers; those who do not are false teachers. The principle Jude sets forth is precisely the same; to them was given the once-for-all deposit of truth.

There can be no timidity about the matter. He must throw all he has into the battle for the safety of the flock.

Seventh, contending vigorously for the faith is not a casual measure that may or may not be taken at one's discretion. Nor is it something that one congregation may be known for, but not another. It is a "necessity," as Jude put it, that should deeply engage the concern of *every* elder in *every* congregation. It is not a matter of advice; it is an inspired command from the Lord to His church through Jude. It is something that all the members of the flock, as well as elders, ought to take to heart. Congregations are vulnerable. They must be defended. Unless the elders conscientiously patrol the borders, these teachers will slip into the tent.

In other words, shepherds must be concerned enough to "watch" (Acts 20:28). Pay attention to this matter. If, after admonition (such as Jude gives), they refuse to do so, either intentionally or by simple neglect, they should be removed from their positions. Too many false teachers gain access by default. How many elders have you ever known to be removed for failing to protect the flock? For that matter, how many elders do you know who have ever been removed for any cause?

So Jude, as a good shepherd of the sheep, instructs us about the problem of false teachers creeping in surreptitiously. I shall not labor the point, but you may read his short epistle and see what he thinks of such persons! If anything, his words are stronger than Paul's, or even the apostle John's. Strong language, such as the apostles use when referring to false teachers, should make it clear that the matter under concern is neither optional nor unimportant. They are using this language to awaken sleepy elders to an important duty that must be met.

Jude gives us some important information about how these teachers worm their way into the hearts of the members of a congregation. Listen to these words:

> *These persons are grumblers, malcontents, who live according to their own desires, and their mouths speak arrogantly, flattering people to gain a favor ... these are persons who cause divisions. They are sensual because they don't have the Spirit (v. 16, 19).*

In these two verses, Jude reveals several characteristics of the false teacher that may alert an elder. One of the principal ways in which false teachers gain an entrance into a congregation and into the good graces of its members is through complaining. He says that they grumble and are malcontents. They pretend to be concerned about problems and soon become advocates for change. That is how they lure the sheep away from their shepherds and win them to their cause. They find something to complain about. And of course, there is always plenty with which to find fault, since neither the elders nor the members are perfect.

Elder-shepherds must always be careful to keep down complaining. The people of Israel constantly got into trouble by listening to and joining in with complainers. The mixed multitude complained, found fault. And this attitude of faultfinding soon swept through the entire congregation of Israel, and rebellion occurred. Paul comments on the sad record of grumbling and its disastrous effects in 1 Corinthians 10:1 through 13. Similarly, in the rebellion of Korah recorded in Numbers 16, we see how complaining about the leadership God had appointed in Israel led to the destruction of many. And even after those tragic events, would you believe it, the people continued to complain (Numbers 15:41 and following)!

By complaining and grumbling about the failures of the present leadership (which, in some cases could have a basis in fact), it is easy to soften up a congregation for the introduction of new ideas and, eventually, new leadership. Because in this life every true believer is dissatisfied with the progress that he is making in his Christian life, it is easy to attribute that to "not being properly fed" by the shepherd of the sheep. Personal responsibility to study Scripture for oneself is largely bypassed. If the charge is true, then something positive must be done to enhance the teaching (feeding) that takes place. Grumbling doesn't fit that category! Prayer for the preacher, sending him to conferences where he can learn more about how to minister, giving him books, and so on, all may help. If nothing does, ruling elders must quietly, kindly, in non-disruptive ways ask him to step down.

Now, above all, elders must not allow a spirit of complaint leading to active grumbling to get a grip on their congregations. That means that, when they detect anything of the sort, they will be Johnny-on-the-spot to do something constructive about it. It means that they will go to the persons who are complaining, tell them of the seriousness of doing so, and point out the relevant Scriptures which show God's displeasure with it. That means they will seek to rectify real wrongs. It means, however, that in serious cases where there is no positive response from the grumbler (even after help is offered), they may have to exercise church discipline—a tool that Jesus Himself placed in the shepherd's bag (see also Matthew 18:15ff.).

Notice that the particular false teachers with whom Jude urged the church to contend were "malcontents." That is to say, nothing—no matter how hard others worked at changing genuinely bad situations—would satisfy them. When people refuse to acknowledge true efforts at reform or growth in a congregation and fail to join positively in the effort, elders should watch out for them. They may be at heart malcontents who like to find fault, who look for problems, who are always punching a hole in the dike but never putting a finger in it to keep water from leaking in. Such people, unless they can be brought to repentance, will do incalculable harm to a congregation. They must not be allowed to continue in this vein.

But Jude also mentions that those about whom he was writing live according to their own desires. Look out for desire and feeling-oriented people. Their thinking and living are not driven by the commandments of God found in the Bible, but by the desires and feelings of their own sinful hearts. When people refuse to acknowledge Scripture as their guide and ignore biblical precepts and examples, they are to be watched. By dragging others down with themselves into the mire that always lies at the end of a desire-and-feeling-oriented life, they may upset entire congregations. This can take place in the area of sex or in as seemingly unrelated areas as one's generally undisciplined lifestyle. Wherever it appears, in whatever form, it is necessary for elders to move in quickly and begin to teach and require disciplined living. Members should not be allowed to do "as they please" (i.e., live according to their desires). The example that they set in a congregation can be devastating to others—especially to young believers and children.

Jude also writes about those who speak "arrogantly." They act as if they are "above" the rest. They are always right. You can't tell them anything. They don't really need any help from the elders. They spout off about anything and everything that comes to mind. There are those who never listen; they always want to speak. When you try to tell them something, before you finish your thought, they have interrupted with thoughts of their own—whether these relate to what you were saying or not. In Proverbs 18:2, such a person is called a "fool." Fools in the book of Proverbs are not merely ignorant, boorish persons; they are also rebellious and arrogant. They are know-it-alls.

Jude also speaks of how divisive persons and heretics gain their way by *flattery*. Pastors themselves are not immune to flattery. A person leaves another church and visits yours. After the first service, he says to your pastor, "I am so glad to be here. What a contrast to the church I have been attending! What good preaching! I can see right away that this is a wonderful place to be," and so on and so forth. Watch out! His enthusiasm may be genuine; all may be aboveboard. But more likely than not, this is mere flattery. A reasonable person doesn't judge on first impressions. He looks more deeply into whatever he is evaluating. At best, the person is superficial, relying on feelings. And we have already seen where that can go! Keep a watch on such a person. Tell him, "I appreciate the fact that you have enjoyed your visit." But soon, you may also have to tell him, "You know, our church is full of sinners who, by His grace, are working on becoming more and more like Christ. There are none here who are perfect. You will find difficulties of every sort. After all, a church is a sort of hospital, or (as Calvin liked to say) a school in which we are all here to learn. None of us has made it yet." His reaction to that sort of explanation may be all-telling.

Jude goes on to speak of the false teachers as "persons who cause divisions." There are good divisions (Luke 12:51) and there are sinful ones (Romans 16:17).[4] Good divisions occur on the basis of biblical principles; sinful ones are based on something else. It can be personality differences,

---

4   Notice how, in this verse, Paul once again urges churches (in particular their elders) to "watch out" for those who by "disregarding the teaching" that was once-for-all given to the saints.

it can be complaining (as we saw above), it can be error (as here in Jude), or almost anything else. Unless there is a truly biblical cause for the division, it is necessary to withstand those who seek to divide Christ's church.

The persons Jude has in mind are, as he says, "sensual because they don't have the Spirit." What he is saying is not necessarily that they are involved in carousing, orgies, and the like, though that may be true. What he has in mind by calling them "sensual" (*psuchikos*, literally "soulish") is that they operate as unbelievers do. The basis for what they think, do, or say is not what the Spirit commands in His Word, but rather, worldly "wisdom." A good commentary on what they are like is found in 1 Corinthians 2, where Paul contrasts the person who has the Spirit with the one who does not. Unbelievers may want to influence your church by making you think they are on the same wavelength as you. They will give you a seemingly reliable profession of faith, but when it comes to living out that faith in decision-making, in attitudes, and in other ways, they will never rely on the Word of God as the basis. They are sensual—worldly.

How does one combat people like this? What should elders do to protect the flock? How should they handle situations in which they failed, and so their congregations are in turmoil? How can they keep the sheep from being mauled? We shall discuss those matters in the next chapter, looking in particular at Jude 20-23.

CHAPTER 16

KEEPING SHEEP FROM BEING MAULED

IN Jude 20-23, God provides specific directions about how to deal with churches that have been set in turmoil by the intrusion of false teaching. Here is what he wrote:

> *But you, dear friends, by building yourselves up in your most holy faith, through praying by the Holy Spirit, keep yourselves in God's love, waiting for the mercy of our Lord Jesus Christ that leads to eternal life. Show mercy to doubters, save others by pulling them out of the fire, and show mercy to others with caution, hating even the clothing spotted by their flesh.*

Here, you will find directions for dealing with three kinds of sheep who have been affected by false teaching. Clearly, the wolf has gotten into the flock Jude addresses. Some sheep are barely alive, being carried off by the wolf, others are just about to be devoured, and still others are in danger's way.

It is instructive that Jude begins by dealing personally with those who are to care for the sheep by contending for the faith. He urges three things:

1. Build yourself up in your most holy faith.
2. Second, pray by the Holy Spirit.
3. Third, keep yourself in God's love.

And all of this is to be done while "waiting for the mercy of our Lord Jesus Christ that leads to eternal life."[1] That is the context for all three of the above endeavors.

---

[1] God's mercy to us ought to remind us to be merciful to erring sheep. Jesus had compassion on people who were like sheep without a shepherd (Mark 7:34). If proper shepherding ministry caused the problem, as it did in the case mentioned in Jude, clearly, compassion must be shown.

Now, what does Jude tell us to do? Unless an elder shepherd knows his "most holy [i.e., separate, unique, one-of-a-kind] faith," it will be impossible for him to contend for it. He must recognize that it is distinct from all other faiths (it is "holy"). That will make him wary of any and all attempts to band together with those of different beliefs. He will not "play footsies" with Rome; he will not engage in "co-belligerency" with Mormons and others. Nor will he allow literature or music to be used in his church that does not conform to Scriptural standards. He will not advise his youth to attend meetings or camps where truth is discounted and emotions and feelings are uppermost. In other words, he will be quite aware of the distinctives of his faith and see to it that in his congregation these distinctives are never watered down, let alone contradicted. On the other hand, he will foster good associations and provide good literature and so on. He will never leave a vacuum for the false teacher to fill.

The ruling elder must know doctrine as thoroughly as the teaching elder in his church.[2] He must know how to present it, how to defend it, and how to show others exegetically where it comes from in the Bible. Otherwise, if he endeavors to contend vigorously for the faith, he will fall flat on his face—and the sheep will see that he is unable to use the rod to defend them. They will wonder, then, whether the false teachers, who seem to know their teachings much better, are not right after all.

In addition, sheep must be patiently, carefully, and fully instructed in their faith so that they will recognize error whenever it appears. It is wise from time to time to hold meetings in which false trends, cults, and other sorts of error are exposed, countered, and refuted. Sometimes, this may most profitably be done by others who are invited in for such purposes, but it is essential for the pastors of a congregation to make the bulk of the presentations so that the flock knows that they have biblical reasons for the hope that is within them. And strong doctrinal teaching is even more essential to the protection of the flock. A flock is comforted by the rod and staff when it is used in these ways!

Then Jude urges prayer. If one has built himself up in his faith, that is good, but it will prove fruitless unless he asks God to use his knowl-

---

2   We presuppose (perhaps wrongly) that the teaching elder does know these things.

edge and understanding to help those who might be deceived. In other words, the whole enterprise of contending for the faith must be done prayerfully. If God is not in it, the effort will be worse than useless—it will be detrimental.

What does it mean to be praying in or by the Holy Spirit? It means that one must willingly submit to His alteration of the prayers that he utters. Paul told us in Romans 8:26 and 27 that the Spirit helps us in our weaknesses. Because we don't always know what to pray for or how to pray (and this might especially be the case in the midst of a congregational disruption), the Spirit may take your prayers and, by shaping them His way, make them more acceptable to God. That means that the answers you receive may not always be to the prayer as you prayed it, but rather, to the prayer as the Holy Spirit molded it! You must be aware of this fact, and be willing to accept with joy whatever He prayed and how the Father answered. God's sovereignty is thus seen even in the matter of His children's prayer life.

Finally, Jude urges us to keep ourselves in God's love. It is always easy during controversy to become nasty instead of loving. Supremely, we must love the sheep because they belong to the One Whom we love supremely—that must be the ruling motive in contending for the faith. No one can contend properly if it is because he loves controversy. More harm than enough has been done in the church because of persons who just like to fight!

Secondarily, love should be shown even for the enemy, hoping that possibly God will bring him to repentance. But we must not have too high hopes and be too easy on him for that reason; the safety of the sheep must come first. Indeed, it is by the clear presentation of the truth of God, as the Spirit uses it, that people are converted, not by seeking to appeal to others by diluting that presentation in any way. The mild—if not cowardly—manners that have been inculcated into the church in our time by some church growth people who never want to offend, and who always want to offer what another is looking for, would not have brought about the Reformation. Those who are captivated by these church growth principles that come out of business strategies ought to read Luther and Calvin and some of the other reformers to get a taste of what it takes to bring about real change.

Love never kept the apostle John—the apostle of love—from calling people liars, antichrists, and so on.[3] Indeed, it is true love to so identify those who are as such. Then, the sheep may know clearly whom to avoid. Indeed, it is the very nature of love for God and for the sheep to be clear, without dulling the truth in any respect. Anything less would not be biblical.

So, Jude is plain. In order to contend vigorously for the faith, you too must be *prepared* to do so. That preparation includes knowing the faith, praying for the venture in all respects, asking the Spirit to make your prayers effectual, and remaining in God's love rather than straying from it in one way or another.

Now, what about the sheep? Well, verses 22 and 23 tell us how to help them. The recipients of Jude's letter were in a situation where wolves had already entered the sheepfold and had carried off some sheep. They were threatening to take others, some of whom were also mauled, and others close to being devoured. Then, there were others who were in danger in the near future. The situation seems to be one of utter havoc.

These three kinds of problems are mentioned. First, there were those who were doubting. They wondered whether or not the false teachers were correct. They were to be treated gently or shown mercy (v. 22). Time and care in pointing out the errors of their ways would be necessary. Mercy here seems to mean gentle, kindly concern and care exhibited to fearful and perplexed sheep. They must be taken out of the fray and dealt with.

Secondly, there were those who were (to use Jude's figure) in the midst of a blazing fire. They must be dealt with differently: you cannot take too long or be so gentle with them—"Pull them out of the fire!" he shouts. You must snatch them from the grasp of the wolf (to return to the shep-

---

3   Jesus called Herod a "fox" and the scribes "hypocrites, whited sepulchers and unwashed cups!" One wonders how the church ever became so effete. The answer is, of course, from fear of embarrassment, ostracism and the like. People like to be liked. While we should not set out to be disliked, we must speak the truth *in love* regardless of the response it elicits.

herdly metaphor) using biblically legitimate means. To do so may require the use of desperate, last-minute action, as the text seems to indicate. It may involve rough handling. It may mean using extraordinary measures.

Lastly, there are those who have already become polluted by the teaching of the false teachers (Jude changes the figure of speech). They have been carried through the muck. And, like helping someone with a loathsome disease whose very clothing is stained with the pus that oozes out upon him, you must not turn from him in disgust, but you must extend mercy to him as you did to the first. Yet, this must be done with "caution" (cf. Galatians 6:1b). The person must not be hated (or loathed) even though he may have polluted himself with the disease of some error. But his clothing, which is spotted with the outcropping of it, *must* be hated and avoided with all "caution." In other words, in helping him (or her), one must be careful not to become defiled himself. The mercy shown here, seemingly, is toward one who has finally recognized the error of his ways and is willing to receive help. All of the words of 2 Corinthians 2:5 through 8 apply to the situation.[4]

Clearly, the circumstance about which Jude was writing need not have occurred. If the elders and the people in the congregation had heeded the warnings set forth in 2 Peter, they would not have allowed these wolves into the sheepfold. They would have fought them off. But, for whatever reason—be it arrogance ("Nothing like that could happen here"), or whatever—they failed. Many churches, likewise, are failing today. It is my hope they will wake up in time. Will you help them do so?

---

4   See comments on this passage in my *The Handbook of Church Discipline.*

CHAPTER 17

TRAINING FOR THE TASK

SHEPHERDING is nothing if it isn't practical. I have already noted that it is no academic exercise. Too many elders attempt to shepherd their flocks in ways that would puzzle a shepherd; ways that—at best—he would find repugnant. Preachers, holed up in their studies, never mixing with their flocks and confronting their enemies, can never shepherd in the ways that Jesus described in John 10, or Paul in Acts 20, or Peter in 1 Peter 5. In all of those places, there is an eminently practical application of truth to the lives of the members of the flock. Shepherding is practical theology at its finest.

Practical theology is often downplayed in sheltered seminaries. The academic side of things is much more strongly asserted. But when a man comes out in the rain, he soon finds that it is the "practical stuff" that he is involved in day by day. His tendency, then, is to retreat to the study, to buy into all sorts of programs that are offered to him, or to radically change his emphasis from the academic to the practical so that he becomes a CEO. None of these responses is biblically appropriate to true shepherding.

In Palestine, younger shepherds learned their trade by going along with older shepherds. They watched, asked questions, were given advice, learned skills, and so on. They became disciples in the fullest sense of the word. That is how seminaries *ought* to teach—but, alas, they do not. Instead, they teach academic subjects—academically. And, for the most part, they teach practical theology academically too! All of that must change in the days to come. But what does one do now? How can he best utilize the existing academic courses to which he is subjected so as to learn how to do the very practical work of shepherding?

Good students who, after graduation, will do a faithful job in days to come rarely concern themselves about grades while in seminary. That is the first fact necessary to learn. They must pass their subjects, of course, but beyond that, they are interested only in obtaining knowledge and skills. That is why they determine not to learn from seminary alone. While attending seminary, they will also take upon themselves some practical tasks in which they will put to work the principles and the practices that they learn in the academic atmosphere of the seminary. Some of them will look for assistant-to-pastor apprenticeships, others will work in a mission, a few will attach themselves to a counseling center, and so on. In one way or another, they will be learning practical skills from others who are engaged in using them.[5]

And—this may make some teachers jittery as they read (if they do)—they will become adept at discovering what it is in the various seminary courses that they attend that is really valuable and, on the other hand, what might just as well be forgotten after the test! Too many academics become so wrapped up in some esoteric concern that they will spend the lion's share of their time studying and teaching it, to the neglect of what is truly important to those who are headed into the ministry. Part of the problem is that too many of the teachers in seminaries have had little or no experience themselves as pastors of churches. They simply don't know what is of importance to shepherding. Worse still, some don't really care! The better pastors are those who, when going through their seminary training, picked and chose what they thought significant to pastoral ministry. They did not allow their teachers to turn them into academics as well. They refused to allow seminary to ruin them!

How does one judge what is important and what isn't? If a student carries on a practical ministry in addition to the academic training that he is getting, he will discover that some of the things he is studying are of greater value to ministry than others. Now, of course, some things may not be immediately useful that would be very valuable to him in the future.[6] But if he is continually asking, "How may I apply this information to the ministry in which I am engaged?" he should soon develop an eye for those things that are (or *will be*) valuable for ministry.

---

5   Some men may find that they cannot sustain both activities at once. That, in itself, may be a test of their call to the ministry, which will demand that they engage in a variety of labor at once.

6   And of course, some facts may not have practical applications, but may orient him biblically.

In other words, since the ideal seminary in which there would be discipling by each teacher does not exist, he must do his best to search out opportunities in which he can "make up for" the lack. There is no substitute for discipling. In it, the older shepherd shows the younger shepherd-to-be the ropes. By answering his questions, making observations, and allowing him to get to know the sheep and their ways, he brings a dimension to his training that is absolutely essential. Somehow, wise students will provide *for themselves* this sort of training that the seminaries currently do not offer. All that shepherding involves—though it may be described on paper and in lectures—cannot be taught academically. A man must come to learn the ways of the sheep and the shepherd who cares for them.

In addition to the seminary students' training, the ruling elders in the flock need to take their personal ministries more seriously. To spend all of their time as a debating society in the confines of a room at the church, and to think that thereby they have discharged the duties of elders, is one of the great mistakes that the elders of many congregations make. Instead, they must constantly deal with people. They must visit, confront when necessary, guide, advise, counsel, and fight for the members of the flock. Elders who only discuss and vote will be a detriment to any congregation. They will be useless when it comes to defending the flock. And they will thwart any preacher who attempts to truly shepherd the people. They must be out among the members of the flock.

Elders, contrary to the seminary student, probably do not have *enough* "academic" training in the Scriptures. In addition to dealing with the flock, they must become earnest students of the Word. They must spend hours with their Bibles and with theology texts that show, systematically and exegetically, how to understand and apply the Scriptures. They should accompany the teaching elder on visits, pray and counsel together with him and with one another, and attend as many courses as possible that are profitable to attend. They, too, must blend the academic with the practical. Any elder who is unwilling to learn—no matter what his age and experience—is not fit to be an elder. All elders must be "teachable" (1 Timothy 3:2).[7]

---

7   There is a dispute about whether the translation should be "apt to teach" or

An eldership that is well taught, Word-and-sheep-oriented, and therefore practical will watch over the flock with great care and concern. They will not allow a wolf even near the flock. They will fight whenever the sheep are attacked, and they will protect them from themselves. They will not neglect the sheep because other matters seem more important to them!

This double emphasis upon the Word and the flock is so essential that whenever it is lost or distorted in one direction or the other, it will cause the flock to suffer. And, within the flock where emphasis is upon the practical, the necessity for protection may not be eclipsed by counseling, visitation, fellowship, or anything else. It too must be a prominent part of eldering ministry.

"teachable." Both are linguistic possibilities. But since the passage speaks mainly of the personal characteristics of the elder, and not his skills, "teachable" seems preferable.

CHAPTER 18

GETTING DOWN TO CASES

How does one employ the rod and the staff to ward off the enemies of the sheep? In passing, I have mentioned various ways in which the implements might be used, but here I want to summarize those a bit and add to them. Naturally, I cannot envision every possible situation, but perhaps it will be helpful to consider a number of the most common ones.

The Mormons are going door-to-door in the community where many of your members live. Should you do anything about it? Most pastors might not. You, however, might take the opportunity to confront the problem head-on. Why not schedule a series of messages on "Mormonism—Its History and Teachings"? Or, perhaps, you might spend one message dealing with Mormonism and follow it with a series of messages on "Doctrines We Believe" (especially setting forth those that conflict with the false doctrines of Mormonism). In one way or another, it is important to use the pulpit that God has given to block the inroads of cults.[1]

Too often the cults gain ground because the flock doesn't know that there is an answer to what they have to say. The elders may announce their willingness to meet with any who have questions and even to schedule a meeting with the Mormon "elders" to discuss the differences between the church and the so-called "Church of Jesus Christ of Latter-day Saints."[2] The elders may prepare a tract exposing the errors of Mormonism and how Mormons may be dealt with when they appear at

---

1 The Mormon door-to-door mission might also be used to evangelize. Prepare a brochure that tells of some of the strange, heretical beliefs of Mormonism. Along with it, explain the way of salvation. Then send members ahead of the twin Mormon "elders" to distribute the pamphlets. As they go from door to door, they may explain that the Mormons are coming and, as a service to the community, your church is handing out these pamphlets that set forth what this cult believes *in contrast to the biblical gospel.*
2 Who now want to be known by the less unusual name "The Church of Jesus Christ."

the door. What we have seen in 2 John should be mentioned in it. These may be distributed to every household in the congregation.

Someone who has mystical tendencies has recently joined your church. At the time when she united with the body, she showed no such leanings, but now, in various ways, they are beginning to manifest themselves. For instance, she goes about the congregation, saying things to other members such as, "Just let go and let God." Or, "The Lord will tell you whether or not you should move." Or, "Learn to listen to God in prayer." Or, "Don't do anything until you have 'peace' about the matter." This sort of activity on her part has begun to have an effect upon others who, following her advice, have begun to make poor decisions based on feelings, hunches, and so on. The congregation, as a result, has become restless. What will you do?

Clearly, you don't want to single this member out from the pulpit (though you may preach a sermon or two on guidance and knowing God's will). What you should do is to confront her personally. You may get nowhere in convincing her that guidance comes only from the Scriptures, or you may be able to help her (and, thereby, bring an end to her advice-giving escapades).

Either way, there is no doubt that either the teaching elder or one of the ruling elders has a responsibility to speak to her about the problem. If, after doing so, she continues to cause unrest in the congregation, she may have to be warned that church discipline will be applied unless she discontinues her "advice-giving." It is one thing for her to be willing to remain quiet while retaining her views and be willing to be taught otherwise, and another to continue to go about upsetting others. If, when dealing with her, she is willing to cease and willing to discuss the matter with the elders, she has a good attitude and should not be subjected to church discipline. But if she persists in disruptive behavior after being confronted and warned, discipline may have to be exercised.

Consider another scenario. Someone visiting your church has handed out tracts to members of your congregation. These tracts teach that God is not sovereign, that man has utter freedom of choice, and that God doesn't know the future. The pamphlets constitute an attack upon your fundamental beliefs about man and God. That visitor, should he show up again at a service, ought to be confronted by an elder and told that he will not be allowed to distribute his materials on the church premises. If he persists, several elders and deacons might tell him that his activities are divisive and, therefore, he is not welcome at the services. It is possible that if he fails to listen to this exhortation to stay away, some deacons might even have to escort him off the church property.

The materials that he has distributed also need to be countered. Possibly, one of the best ways to do this is to publish a response and hand it out to each member. Mention of the problem may be made from the pulpit, and if serious enough, a refutation of the errors that are presented may be given. Clearly, in one way or another, the charges that have been leveled against biblical truth must be countered.

Take another situation. There is a heretical teacher across town who has a radio broadcast that has captured the attention of a number of your members. You hear about their interest from a member who has begun to question some of the doctrines of the faith (perhaps the doctrine of eternal punishment, for example). Inquiring about this further, you discover that several families have been listening regularly to his teachings. What will you do about it?

It might be necessary to find out how many families are affected and who they are, and then plan to meet jointly with them. In this meeting, the families and the elders might discuss the matters at issue so as to inform the members about the errors that they have been imbibing. These must be soundly refuted, and the opposing truths must be clearly set forth. In convening the meeting, it will be necessary to explain the importance of protecting the flock. Let them know that it is not rivalry that is behind the meeting, but a love for the truth of God and for them.

How about that local "Christian" bookstore on the other side of town in which all sorts of weird, wild, and heretical teachings may be found? Well, the answer to that problem is to start a congregational book service of your own in which you monitor every volume that is sold. If you sell, not for profit, but to make good books available, you will keep your members away from the mine field of error on the shelves of that store across town. There should be no reason for your sheep to stray across town if your store is well-stocked. In addition to the convenience of a store at the church, such a congregational bookstore encourages members to read helpful Christian literature. Moreover, there are those who will not go across town to buy a book under any circumstances, who will be glad to be able to get them at church.

Then, there are the materials that you use in your church—not only Church School quarterlies, and so forth, but tracts in the rack and the literature on the table in the narthex. If you don't provide good written information, members of the congregation are liable to obtain doubtful materials elsewhere. It is worth investing some money in such reading materials so that there will be an abundance on all sorts of subjects. Especially, there should be pamphlets setting out the principal doctrines of the Bible.

Here's another possibility. There are those who are disgruntled in the congregation. They are grousing about the Church School, about the preacher, about the music, about the youth group, about the "deadness" in the church. Now, if there is a serious reason to find fault, the elders ought to do two things: first, they should thank the member who is complaining for pointing out the problem that they raised. Then they should assure them that something will be done to rectify it (and, sure enough, they must follow through on that promise). But after doing so, if they find the person still grousing, they must confront him about his attitude. And if he is one who is always complaining about everything—no matter how trivial the difficulty—they may have to speak to him about that matter too. In one way or another, as we have seen, the destruction from grumbling that beset the Israelites and the early church must be remembered—and avoided!

Some people may infect an entire congregation by their defeatist attitudes. If they are always throwing cold water on everything, handing out dire predictions of failure and the like, their attitudes must be challenged. Discouragement, once it has gotten a hold, can eat away at the vitals of any congregation. The elders must take out their staffs, dust them off, and counsel them about their attitudes, giving them the biblical perspective. Which is? Namely this: we are pessimistic about what the world is doing or may do, but we are entirely optimistic about what God is doing, or may do. And the latter, being true, should far overshadow the former so as to bring hope and joy to the believer even in the midst of seeming defeat. Counseling defeated Christians is essential.

These are only a few of many possible occurrences that elders will regularly face in their congregations, to which they must be alert and to which they should bring their rods and staffs to rectify. Largely, the staff will be used first, especially when dealing with members, but the rod may sometimes have to follow. With those who seek to disrupt the flock, often from the outset, it is the rod alone that is appropriate. When, and only when, an eldership is active and responsive to what is happening to the flock, will wolves and bears be vanquished and the sheep comforted.

CHAPTER 19
NOW IT'S YOUR TURN

U SING the examples given in the previous chapter, together with the biblical principles set forth in this book, consider what you would do were you to become involved in the following scenarios. I suggest that in no more than five sentences you describe the action you would take.

1. Two members of your congregation have been meeting regularly for personal Bible study during their lunch hours. This study, as you learn from the teacher of their Church School class, has resulted in a growing belief (now a conviction) that Jesus Christ will visibly return to this earth on a specific date. They are now telling others in the congregation about their "discovery" and urging them to prepare for the event. "Preparation" includes financing an effort to publicize the supposed "good news" through radio, TV, and newspaper advertisements in order to propagate these beliefs and raise more funds for additional publicity. How will you respond?

2. Jane, a former prostitute, is converted and seems to be growing in her faith. Several months after joining the church, Sally reports to the pastor that Jane has been soliciting some of the married men in the church who are too embarrassed to reveal the fact. You are uncertain about this report because Sally has been known to spread gossip before. As an elder, what actions would you be sure to take?

3. A family in your congregation has had a Jehovah's Witness call upon them. Evidently, he denied Christ's deity, and John, the husband in the family, is wondering whether or not what he said is true. A second visit by the cultist is scheduled for next week. John's wife, Barbara, is concerned about developments and has appealed to the pastor for help. You are the pastor. What will you do?

4. One of the elders of your church, who has been conducting a home Bible study on behalf of the congregation, suddenly announces that he intends to take a dozen or more of the members of the Bible study and start a church with himself as their pastor. This divisive action must be dealt with quickly according to Titus 3:10. The perpetrator of this schism must be confronted. But how? Can those sheep he has influenced be retrieved? If so, how?

5. From comments made by several members of your congregation, you learn that a considerable number of your members listen to Benny Hinn on a more-or-less regular basis. This is disturbing since Hinn has taught heresy, is notorious for false miraculous healings, and prophecies that could seriously jeopardize their Christian experience. It is alleged that one family, in particular, has given the impetus to this activity. Will you do something to protect the flock? If so, what? You are an elder.

If you have been able to respond to these questions in ways that seem adequate, good! If, on the other hand, you are perplexed as to what to do or say, perhaps you should read the book again. It may be profitable to discuss these matters in your elders' meeting. Forewarned is forearmed.

CHAPTER 20

CONCLUSION

THE burden of this book has been to alert the church to the fundamental reason why so much has gone wrong with the church, so often and in so many ways. I have maintained that if the eldership that is in charge of the churches had faithfully discharged its shepherdly duties over the centuries, we would have had far less defection, far fewer errors, and far more progress in spreading the gospel throughout the world. And, in particular, the essential shepherdly duty that has been all but abrogated today (as well as in the past) is the protection of the flock against the wolves.

From the multiplicity of passages to which I have referred in the New Testament, it should be evident that Jesus and the apostles knew that there would be heretics, cultists, divisive persons, and the like who would slip into the church in order to do her damage. They spoke of them as wolves and bears and strongly urged shepherd-elders to be alert and on guard against their intrusion. To them was given the staff of admonition and counsel, the rod of destruction and discipline, and the pulpit and the computer with which to ward them off.

The eldership has, in almost every generation, failed miserably. But it is not necessary for that to happen. Not only are the Scriptures replete with warnings against letting the guard down, but they also explain how to fight effectively. God has given the rod, together with elder-authority, to do so.

So far as I know, there is no other book that sets forth the need for elders to use their rods and staffs. If this volume serves its purpose at all, it will be a call to awaken those who ought to be standing guard. I pray that it will be.

www.ingramcontent.com/pod-product-compliance
Lightning Source LLC
LaVergne TN
LVHW051235080426
835513LV00016B/1595